The Crabby
Chronicles

The Crabby Angels Chronicles

✦

Radical Guidance on Love, Healing, Happiness, Inner Peace and Creating Miracles in Everyday Life.

Jacob Glass

BASED ON THE PRINCIPLES OF
A COURSE IN MIRACLES

iUniverse, Inc.
New York   Bloomington

The Crabby Angels Chronicles
Radical Guidance on Love, Healing, Happiness, Inner Peace and Creating Miracles in Everyday Life

iUniverse books may be ordered through booksellers or by contacting:

iUniverse
1663 Liberty Drive
Bloomington, IN 47403
www.iuniverse.com
1-800-Authors (1-800-288-4677)

Because of the dynamic nature of the Internet, any Web addresses or links contained in this book may have changed since publication and may no longer be valid.

ISBN: 978-1-4502-0603-7 (sc)
ISBN: 978-1-4502-0605-1 (dj)
ISBN: 978-1-4502-0604-4 (ebk)

Printed in the United States of America

iUniverse rev. date: 01/20/10

With great honor and gratitude to the three graces:
Helen Schucman
Marianne Williamson
Diane Meyer-Simon

Epigraph:

There is no order of difficulty in miracles. One is not "harder" or "bigger" than another. They are all the same. All expressions of love are maximal.

--A Course in Miracles

Introduction

○ ○

The Call is universal. It goes on all the time everywhere . . . many hear It, but few will answer. Yet it is all a matter of time. Everyone will answer in the end, but the end can be a long, long way off. . . And each one saves a thousand years of time as the world judges it. To the Call Itself time has no meaning.

-A Course in Miracles

I was drafted by God (or the Universe, or Source, or the Divine Mother or whatever it is that *you* call the Great It). I'm mostly comfortable with the word God so that's what I'll use here as we get to know each other a little bit. Anyhow, God came and got me a long-ass time ago.

First it was to be a Catholic altar boy for daily mass at Catholic school. Later when I was in the third grade, the priest came to my home-room in the morning asking the teacher for a boy who could read well. Again, I was forcibly volunteered for the job.

In High School I was made chaplain of the FBLA club, though I think they may have specifically made up that position for me. And it's not as though I went around talking about God or praying in public. I think that people just felt THEM around me. More about Them in a bit. At the Mormon college I attended as an acting major, I was actually sought out by directors of various plays to play missionaries, angels, and unborn spirits, in spite of the fact that I was not a particularly talented actor.

Naturally, all I really wanted to be was "normal" like the Brady Bunch and those other all-American families on TV. But the truth is, I was abundantly weird, dressing in capes, scarves and hats, in fact dressing as if life were a continuous costume drama, reading books on self-hypnosis, using crystal balls, having séances, and surrounded by Catholic religious icons at home. I even had a beautiful hand-made altar that my father made with candle holders, a crucifix, holy water. Basically, I was prepared to give the last rites on a moment's notice. I don't think Keith Partridge had any of that stuff.

In hindsight I can now see that my life actually *was* a typically all-American unit in that it was full of real human beings with issues that were not all that funny at the time. No need to go into the "story" but suffice to say I had a wonderfully dysfunctional family with a lovingly irresponsible alcoholic father and a creatively talented but stifled, depressed and sometimes enraged mother. We lived in constant economic and emotional highs and lows and all of this made me wildly nervous and full of psychosomatic illnesses and panic attacks.

I just wanted to marry Marie Osmond, have 20 kids and live my life inside one of their family Christmas specials. Of course, inside I knew this was problematic for all the reasons you might imagine, but in particular since I was so obviously gay in that most of my crushes had been on the cute guys I'd see on TV. Religion, God, sexuality, wanting to fit in and being quite odd and having an odd family . . . my plan was falling to shit all the time in every way imaginable.

Plus, even after I let go of my fantasy of living a heterosexualized 1970's sitcom life, God kept stalking me to do meaningful spiritual work. By now, all I wanted was to look cute, wear designer clothes and become a famous actor who people wanted to sleep with. I was definitely wading in the shallow end of the pool and not a good candidate for a deeper calling of service and spiritual instruction. Yet, I kept right on ending up doing exactly that, time after time.

One of my first jobs after graduating high school was working as a clerk at a Benedictine monastery where I helped in the mail program for those who wrote in to have Mass said for their dear departed loved ones. This was a job I never applied for at a place I'd never heard of before. I received a phone call from the priest who ran the place who said that someone, he couldn't remember who, had given him my name and phone number and said I could type. Shit like this happens to me all the time.

There are so many more stories like that which lead up to the writing of this book and perhaps one day we'll sit down and if you really care I'll tell them to you. But you're buying the drinks.

Suffice to say I've been avoiding writing this book my whole life. I've been lecturing full-time on spirituality and specifically on *A Course in Miracles* for nearly 20 years and have been a little bit embarrassed by it for much of that time. For so long there were still those remnants of wanting to be "normal" and yet my life is always totally out of step with the "normal" world around me. I did not achieve any of the things that I set out to do or that I thought were so very important and necessary for my happiness and it's taken a very long time to let that go and accept the life I actually have. And I can honestly say that my life is very rewarding and I love what I do, the students and people I interact with and I pinch myself every day that I get to do something that I love so much.

Now I not only accept my weirdness, I celebrate it. I get a kick out of the people who call me the "miracle guy" and who say that I'm the guy who has angels and spirit guides talking to him all the time. It's fine that I'm the one who people are drawn to come sit down with, completely uninvited as they pour out the secrets they've never told anyone when what I am really interested in talking about is how sexy Jon Hamm was on Mad Men last night.

Also, I don't even fit into the "new thought" group of teachers because I'm not sweet, I love to swear and I still have a plate full of character defects I'm working on. And to be honest, I still don't advertise my lectures and often actively discourage people from coming to them because I tend to teach like a drill sergeant running a spiritual boot camp and not everyone is quite up to that kind of intensity. My groups are like a badly kept secret though. Best-selling authors like Marianne Williamson and Debbie Ford and others have come and lectured with me. Grammy winner Kenny Loggins has come and sung on my stage. Celebrities, nuns, priests, Zen monks, rabbis, politicians and authors – they've all found me and come to hear me or sought me out for private counseling and yet you've probably never heard of me and most churches and new thought publishers won't come near me with a 10 foot pole. That's totally cool with me. I actually LIKE being the weirdo now. I've stopped resisting who I am and what I came here to do.

So this is the book my fabulous nutty funny loving stalker angels wanted me to give to you. They've been after me for so long and I am old and cranky enough now to not really care what the world or anyone in it thinks of me anymore so I thought, ah why not let em write Their book now? They're a nutty bunch who fit my life perfectly. They come in all shapes and sizes, from the sexy half-dressed Giant Angels who look like they were cast in Hollywood to the Brotherhood who all wear Hawaiian shirts and are always drinking and wanting to have a party to . . . well, there are a LOT of different types and They needed a particularly odd fellow to send their lessons through. Like me, they speak in the modern language, enjoy swearing and can be rather blunt at times. I love Them and they take good care of me. It's been a joy writing it and I hope you will find it a joy to read.

p.s. I had no idea what to name this book and I was a little blocked in hearing what the Guides were giving me because I get so nervous about naming things - so my friend Dana received the title in one of her daily meditations. It really just seemed to fit though to be honest I am probably more crabby than the Angels and Guides ever are. And it's a chronicle because these lessons were originally written one-a-day over a 6 month period and were posted online for people to read as a daily teaching. I don't take myself very seriously and so it seemed ridiculous to have a "serious" spiritual title for this book. So, I'm grateful that Dana had her ears open for the Guides when I could not quite hear clearly.

So, you better watch out too – the air is thick with angels and guides who all have a good and holy purpose to be fulfilled through us all. And if you are really open and pay attention, you may find that they are pretty funny and amazingly entertaining companions here on this beautiful crazy fucked up planet.

Preface

○ ○

The Holy Spirit's Voice is as loud as your willingness to listen.

-A Course in Miracles

I call this a "spiritual plop book." It is here as one of the tools in your spiritual tool box to help you find your own answers from the Voice within. We all have our own unique path and there is no "one size fits all" path. This book is a bit unique also in that it was not written for you to read in order from the beginning to the end unless you feel moved to do so.

So many times when we are seeking guidance we've received direction from some "random" thing we saw on TV, words in a song that was playing at the time, something a friend casually mentions, and even from a bumper sticker on the car in front of us.

Well, this book is another way to seek Guidance and direction from the Universe. I suggest that you simply "plop" the book open to a page and let whatever is there penetrate your consciousness either as your lesson for that day, or if seeking a specific answer you can say a prayer, ask for Help or ask a sincere question and then "plop" the book open and let Spirit speak to you as you might with the I Ching or the Runes or any other tool for divination. Ruminate on what you read, see if it feels right for you and ask God or Source to help you have a discerning spirit. Remember, YOU are the authority in your life and you must never renounce that responsibility to a book, a spiritual organization, a person or a teaching.

1

There is Nothing Wrong With You

○ ○

You are the work of God, and His work is wholly lovable and wholly loving. That is how one must think of himself in his heart because that is what he is.

-A Course in Miracles

We are asking you to resist the temptation to "hit the ground running" today with self-initiated plans and strategies of self-improvement. The self that you want to improve does not exist at all except within a story that you tell yourself and it is Our desire that this be a year in which Reality replaces all limiting stories. This is a year of miracles. This is the year you have been asking for. It is a time for you to deepen your relationship with the Self that God made.

It's true that your personality may need some Guidance and Correction along the way but it is best if you leave that to Us. You should be greatly relieved that it is not up to you to change yourself since so many of your past attempts have failed or failed to last. Rather, be willing for your mind to be changed and the personality self will become simply another means of reaching other minds in love. This is a year in which you will perform miracles with great regularity and We are so grateful to you for doing your part in the Great Campaign of restoring the awareness of Love to all minds. Remember that the motto of the Campaign is "Listen, Learn and DO." Let Us add now as an addendum to that . . . "joyfully." It is Our desire that you learn to see yourself as a joyful Miracle Worker rather than as a separate little ego self struggling to become perfect.

If there are things that you desire to experience in this new year, give it to Us that We may purify your thoughts around it and remove all traces of fear and anxiety. Nothing truly beneficial is ever withheld from you when you join with Us – in fact, only you are capable of withholding anything from you. And you are wiser than you think you are. Call to mind now 3 things that are desires of your heart for this year and say them out loud if you are in private.

Now together let Us give them to the Holy Spirit so that we may release motivation and have it be replaced with Divine Inspiration:

Dear God, I offer now to You all the dreams, goals and intentions of my heart. Please heal my mind of all fearful thoughts and stressful concepts as I now open to Your Guidance. There is nothing I want to get, I want only to receive the bounty of blessings You have chosen for me. I will not worry nor interfere with Your Plan but offer my hands, feet and voice to do whatever You will for me to do today and throughout the year. I walk in joyful faith today! Amen

2

The Way You Describe the Problem IS the Problem

True denial is a powerful protective device. You can and should deny any belief that error can hurt you.

-A Course in Miracles

Don't be so reasonable all the time. Miracles are totally unreasonable to the ego mind whereas pain, lack and limitation make perfect sense to it. The miracle worker makes little progress if she is going to spend most of her time focusing on the problem and all of its various facets and aspects. Progress comes from focus on solutions.

Your early metaphysicians knew the power of positive denial. They denied evil, denied sickness, and denied darkness as anything other than appearances. One of your great actresses Ruth Gordon always said, "Never face the facts!" Remember that to teach is to demonstrate. She was a miracle worker who taught through her demonstration that the only obstacles are the ones you believe in. Her greatest career successes came in spite of all the facts and came quite late in life – her body, her age, her voice, her demeanor were all obstacles to everyone but her. Everyone is free to focus on whatever they choose – and their focus becomes their reality. A miracle is a shift in focus; a shift in perception, another way of looking at things. It is a decision to keep the mind open and relaxed.

A miracle worker is one who has begun describing the Answer rather than the problem. As you describe a problem, you tend to make it solid, real and you box yourself in as you talk about it more and more. In fact, you often depress and terrify yourself and THEN ask for a miracle. God does not interfere with your own creations so if you terrify yourself then your creation is terror and YOU are the one who must stop you.

Many of you like to use the phrase "think outside of the box" but notice you've still created a box in this scenario. You terrify yourself and then try to manifest courage to overcome it. Instead realize that THERE IS NO BOX! It is another illusion to be denied. Break the habit of describing problems and cultivate a new habit of describing the Answer even though the specifics of it are yet unknown. General statements of faith are the seeds you sow:

"God is with me now. He has a plan for my life. There is no need to worry or rush. The Universe has perfect timing. All that I need to know is being revealed to me."

3

Do Not Compare and Despair

o o o o o o o o o o o o o o o o o o o o o o o o o o o o o o o o o o o o

You are not making use of this course if you insist on using means which have served others well, neglecting what was made for you.

-A Course in Miracles

To be inspired is "of the Spirit" and is a primary means of communication from Us to you. However you can count too heavily on looking to others for inspiration. The danger in this is the ego's tendency to take the initial experience of being inspired by another and then perverting it into comparison with someone you judge as somehow better or better off. Instead, simply look at them, and silently say, "Good for them" and then return to your own yard.

Remember this is a highly individualized curriculum. No one else has the exact same set of lessons, skills, gifts or potential that you do. One of the greatest lessons of the miracle worker is to learn to live without the external approval of the world, not because it will not come but because it is ephemeral when it does come. Your job is to fulfill YOUR function in YOUR way.

If you find that you are inspired by the actions of another person and it uplifts you to the Christ vibration then by all means begin to walk in that direction with full understanding that even if you do

EXACTLY what they did, it will still look different in your life. But, if it begins to create anxiety, stress, competition and comparisons, then you have taken the detour into fear and have left your own unique path of Light and then return to your highlighted route.

Remember too that you are an ever-evolving student. What worked for you yesterday may not work today so the means which served the you of Monday may not serve the you of Wednesday. This causes distress to those who cling to the illusion of stability. Remember that the Buddha taught that you suffer because of your attachment to permanency in an ever-changing physical impermanent world.

Do not compare yourself with others. Do not compare yourself with who you were yesterday. Do not compare yourself with an idealized fantasy of who you think you should be. Today, be open to Divine Guidance of your now. Affirm:

I will not judge my unique path today. I am always in the right place at the right time and MY good is beyond comparison. My part in God's plan is perfect for ME.

4

Seek Only What You Want to Find

○ ○

What you acknowledge in your brother you are acknowledging in yourself, and what you share you strengthen.

-A Course in Miracles

Too often you are unconsciously seeking within others the things that will only make you feel disconnected from God, depressed, angry, afraid and guilty should you find them. When you focus your attention on the faults of those around you, you activate those very same qualities within yourself, even if you suppress and deny they are there. In fact, they may be things that YOU would never act upon, or things that you feel you have "conquered" within yourself and in these cases your projection of attack thoughts will be even more intense. However, YOU are the one who will suffer as a result of these attack thoughts. They will go on with their day perfectly unaffected by your thoughts.

It is far better for your health in every dimension to seek the qualities in others that you WANT to find because you will also be strengthening those qualities within yourself. Try to remember that there is no such thing as constructive criticism. All attack thoughts are destructive to the one thinking them and attack thoughts never leave your own mind. You cannot get rid of them by sharing them. Instead, surrender them to the Holy Spirit and ask that your mind be corrected and healed.

As you choose today to focus on only the loving qualities in those who enter your awareness, you will find that your self-perception will also become kinder and more generous. To intensify the process and reap even greater rewards, verbally acknowledge the good that you see in others. Practice telling others what is wonderful about them all day today and by the evening your heart will be full of joy, love and a feeling of deep accomplishment.

5

Practice Being a Nobody

o o o o o o o o o o o o o o o o o o o o o o o o o o o o o o o

*The body's serial adventures, from the time of birth to dying are
the theme of every dream the world has ever had.*

- A Course in Miracles

The ego will use even so-called spirituality as a way to aggrandize and
set itself apart as a path to subtle and not-so-subtle suffering. Too
often you tend to want to become rather than to BE. And much of the
world's commerce is based on easily manipulating you because of your
addiction to being noticed, being accepted, being liked, being worthy,
being supported, being acknowledged - setting yourself apart in some
way that you feel is unique and special. "Special" is a code word for
tormented and insane. Even the belief that you are so much worse than
other people is an egoic attempt to establish specialness.

The ego's greatest fear is not only that you are powerful beyond
measure, for this is an idea that it quickly uses against you. The greatest
fear of the modern ego is that you are just like everyone else. In fact
in your world, one of the most insulting things you can call someone
is average, unexceptional or ordinary. Yet, if you really considered
the moments when you've experienced the greatest inner-peace and
contentment it is usually in those moments of your deepest humility.
This is why people yearn to connect with nature - because in the
presence of nature there is no one and nothing to impress. Compared

to the ocean and the mountains you are lost in the thrilling rush of the insignificance of personality.

This is not a practice to do for long periods of time because it is liable to move from peace to discomfort if held too long. What We are advocating is something as brief as 30 seconds to 5 minutes, 3 times a day during which you simply stop the inner-narration of the story of "you" - drop explaining yourself, describing yourself, auditioning for approval - drop your titles of mother, man, boss - and even your descriptions such as spiritual, funny, intelligent. For 30 seconds just sit down, shut up and receive.

"The meek shall inherit the earth because their egos are humble, and this gives them truer perception."

--A Course in Miracles

6

Thinking of You, Wish You Would Change

o o o o o o o o o o o o o o o o o o o o o o o o o o o o o o o o o o o

The ego's plan for salvation centers around holding grievances. It maintains that, if someone else spoke or acted differently, if some external circumstance or event were changed, you would be saved. Thus, the source of salvation is constantly perceived as outside yourself.

- A Course in Miracles

In the ego's "special relationship" the participants are always working on the relationship, trying to dominate, manipulate and control the other person into meeting their endless abyss of ever-changing needs. In the Holy Relationship, there is nothing to work on except your own perceptions - and this is done by turning them over to the Holy Spirit.

When a mind is truly transformed by the Light, behavior will follow. You have reversed cause and effect by thinking that behaviors will change thoughts. In this way you are always at war with your own mind and with the behaviors of those around you. Perhaps if you recognized how often you have failed to change your own behaviors on a permanent peaceful basis you will see why it is so pointless to put yourself in charge of changing others.

Instead, be willing today to truly "live and let live" as you offer all of your thoughts and concepts about other people and the world to the Holy Spirit. If there is someone or something in particular which throughout the day worries, upsets or in any way disturbs you, remember the advice of your grade school teacher who admonished you to "keep your eyes on your own paper!" We use you to change others in positive ways quite frequently - but you are almost always totally unaware of it at the time. The more YOU try to change others, the more stubbornly they will resist. As you release others to Divine Care, they are more likely to be inspired to their next level of freedom and peace. Be less ambitious and more willing and all will unfold in perfect divine order.

7

"Fuck You My Brother"

○ ○

Let us not forget, however, that words are but symbols of symbols.
They are thus twice removed from reality.

- A Course in Miracles

Try to remember that the ego will make every attempt to use against
you what God meant for good. And there is nothing that has been used
against you with more damage and suffering than the word "love."
People do all kinds of insane things in the name of love and it is most
often used as a way to separate, tyrannize and manipulate yourself and
others. It is thought of as an emotion rather than recognized as a state
of being which cannot be altered. Love does not need to be invoked,
but rather recognized as already present.

Our dear Brother Jacob discovered this some time ago as he
struggled to see the innocence in others. As he tried valiantly to follow
Jesus' entreaty to love others, he grew to resent them more than ever.
As with most of you, he thought it would be easier to love others if
they would simply be more lovable. On the sidewalks of Los Angeles
he would try to practice love by mentally greeting each person with an
inner "Namaste'" - trying to see the Christ and Buddha in everyone.
Instead of bringing peace is simply amplified his own feelings of guilt
over the endless judgements that arose from within him as he failed
over and over again.

It was his concept of "love" which got in the way. We encouraged him to simply silently greet each person with "Fuck you my brother-fuck you my sister" instead. Immediately a lightness came over him as he began to laugh at his own ego thoughts and in that moment he felt his one-ness with every person who he saw and his heart opened wide. Infinite love is not about the words or your concepts of what "spiritual" looks like - it is an experience.

You can indeed afford to laugh at fear thoughts, remembering that God goes with you wherever you go.

- A Course in Miracles

8

Marinated in Love

So many of your prayers and concerns are about filling some perceived lack or gap, healing something you think is broken, fixing some illusory problem. But really these are all just symptoms of the one and only problem which is that you've forgotten how much We love you. This more than a greeting card sentiment, it is more than saccharine mush.

YOU ARE LOVED BY ALL THAT IS AND THE CREATOR OF ALL THAT IS. Yes, YOU . . . in all of your self-identified faults and "character defects" - exactly the way you are.

And never for one single moment do you walk alone in this life, never. Never is there a moment that you are not surrounded, not just by a cosmic impersonal love but by US in our etheric forms and formlessness seeing you exactly where and how you are in this moment. We know you intimately and have been with you since your physical entrance into this world. You can call us angels or guides, spirits or even fairies if it pleases you - the mystics and seers from the beginning of time have told you about Us. Your poets and story tellers and artists have never forgotten us, but you forget quite frequently and then seek in the silliest places for "magic" when the air is already thick with miracles.

Ruminate on Our love for you in the coming days - meditate on it, look for the signs of it. When you have a prayer that reflects some worry, some fear, some sense of lack or brokenness, STOP and try to feel Our love right then and there. Envision us flying alongside your car with you, and as you walk down the street . . . you may think this silly and yet you don't think it silly when you envision future catastrophes in your life that are completely fictional. We are as real to you as you will allow us to be and once you begin to grow in that faith walk, you will see evidence of Us everywhere. So rather than focus on your need today, you might try to focus on allowing in Our love for you instead, no matter what the problem or need seems to be.

"If you knew Who walks beside you on the way that you have chosen, fear would be impossible."

- A Course in Miracles

9

Divine Discomfort

We are very well aware of the "divine discomfort" that you are feeling lately. This is very different than a discomfort coming from "something wrong" going on in your world. Cause and effect are always at work and you are feeling the effects of a prayerful cause that you yourself set in motion. Can you see that the earth people are all in a growing season which many are very resistant to because they see it as a discomfort that is "wrong" somehow. People are scrambling in an effort to NOT change and this goes against the whole movement of the Universe itself.

It IS true that when you ask it is given, but YOU must be in a place of receiving what is asked for. Too often you think that you will ask and the answer will simply arrive in an effortless joyful manner because of the times in your past when this has happened. However, in those situations what you asked for was the next logical step for you and no change in YOU was necessary. This is not the case now as you have been asking for life experiences that necessitated changes in YOU and the way you live your days and nights.

This is a growing season and there are bound to be "growing pains" - those aches that come from being stretched. We are asking you to do your best to soothe yourself through those moments and most of all, do not resist or think that something is wrong even if you feel the need for a good cry or a temper tantrum. Everything is quite right in fact. Do not try to take control of the situation or make it an enemy and do not even attempt to do this perfectly. We would be surprised if you were NOT feeling awkward at a time like this. An awkward stage always precedes a new level of self-mastery.

Please remember that it is not YOUR job to purify yourself, We are the Great Purifier. Let Us handle whatever messes may surround you and WE will surround you with all the Help you need.

> *The next stage is indeed "a period of unsettling." Now must the teacher of God understand that he did not know what was valuable and what was valueless. All he really learned so far was that he did not want what was valueless . . . he must learn to lay all judgment aside, and ask only what he really wants in every circumstance. Were not each step in this direction so heavily reinforced, it would be hard indeed!"*

-A Course in Miracles

10

Don't Believe Everything You Think

o o o o o o o o o o o o o o o o o o o o o o o o o o o o o o o o

No evidence will convince you of the truth of what you do not want.

-A Course in Miracles

The misguided attempt to try to control the mind is very frustrating. Try to remember that there is no need to control your thoughts but rather that it is much better to gently become aware of them so that they can be dealt with properly. The real problem is not all of the disturbing thoughts that you have but that you believe them so readily. And what you think and believe you will see even if it is not really there. Mind always proves itself right. It is the job of mind to gather evidence of whatever it believes to be true.

For instance, if you have thoughts of unworthiness and you believe those thoughts, then no matter how much love is showered upon you, you will see a world that rejects you. The ego does not want your happiness or peace so it will always attempt to amplify fear thoughts and will then go about gathering evidence to prove its case. But do not forget that no matter how much evidence of guilt you may have, in the end the Higher Court will dismiss the case!

Many many thoughts will run through your mind today and the vast majority of them will be old thoughts – things you have thought many times before. If you do not like what you are thinking, rather than try to get rid of the thought, bring it into the Light and question it. YOU DO NOT HAVE TO BELIEVE YOUR THOUGHTS. YOU CAN CHOOSE AND CHOOSE YOU MUST if you want to be free from even minor suffering.

Remember the Byron Katie teachings – write out any disturbing thoughts and then question those thoughts as you ask, "Can I absolutely KNOW that this is true? Who would I be without these thoughts?" Then, give all your thoughts to Brother Jesus. Surrender them all in prayer as you ask the Holy Spirit to purify your mind and restore you to sanity, joy, and inner peace.

11

Assume the Best

o o o o o o o o o o o o o o o o o o o o o o o o o o o o o o o

You do not ask too much of life, but far too little. When you let your mind be drawn to bodily concerns, to things you buy, to eminence as valued by the world, you ask for sorrow, not for happiness.

-A Course in Miracles

Walk through your day today KNOWING that divine Aid is with you – that your day is already unfolding in perfect divine order before you even ask. Your part today is to not to let your self-initiated plans and tendency to try to control interfere with the flow of Tao today. We urge you to drink from the Living Waters by opening your mind and softening your heart. This is a matter of intention and willingness. We are exercising your faith muscle today. Practice being a gracious receiver today. Remember that a "get" mentality is not a receptive mentality. Be receptive today. Slow down, breathe, relax, let go.

Assuming the best does not mean that all the desires of the ego will be met or that you will get what you want if what you want is something external. It is good to remember that the ego is insatiable in its desires. "Princes, palaces and parking spaces" is the "best" that the ego seeks because these are forms that distract you from content so that you will continue to consume without meeting your real nutritional needs. Many of the most insatiable consumers are actually starving to death emotionally because they are not being nourished by all their "stuff." The forms of the world are neutral. They are neither good nor bad. What gives them meaning is which part of the mind is using them. But of themselves, they are incapable of nourishing or satisfying you.

Assuming the best is about the content of your day and not the form it takes. Let yourself be nourished today recognizing that the Holy Spirit wants what is best for you and knows exactly how and when to deliver all good in perfect order and timing.

Don't think about what could go wrong today; be open to what could go right.

Think possibilities rather than probabilities today. Remember that "lots can happen" and you do not need to know how. As you assume the best today you are aligning yourself with the Force that holds galaxies in place.

12

Vibrational Clean-up on Aisle Four

o o o o o o o o o o o o o o o o o o o o o o o o o o o o o o o o o o o o

You are much too tolerant of mind wandering, and are passively condoning your mind's miscreations.

-A Course in Miracles

How have your thoughts been? Are you loving them? If not, then it's time to clean up the old vibration. Every thought is a vibration of love or fear and it attracts to it similar vibrations or matching thoughts. Whatever you have been thinking creates a momentum and it is easier to keep thinking in whatever direction you've been thinking. Yes, it is so easy to backslide into old patterns of fear, but it is actually just as easy to backslide into positive patterns by now too. The more you practice gently guiding your thoughts each day, the better you will become at it and the more cooperative your mind will be.

No one has a good mind or a bad mind. The mind is like a puppy – it is trained or untrained. Just as one would not passively allow a puppy to destroy the peace of your home through destructive chewing, biting, barking, and relieving itself everywhere, you must also not be passive when it comes to your own thoughts. The mind is a wonderful companion and friend but a horrible master. Never make an enemy of your mind and do not feel guilty because of your thoughts. Instead, cultivate an attitude of patient consistency in dealing with your mind. Reward yourself for every step forward with self-talk words of encouragement and support.

Your emotions will always tell you when you have allowed in a thought or series of thoughts that are not in alignment with the Divine Truth, because you will not be feeling peaceful or happy. When that happens CHOOSE how you WANT to feel then ask for Guidance as you ask this question "What could I think that would help me feel the way I want to feel?"

Remember, you can always reach for a better feeling thought. You don't need to go for the highest most optimistic loving thought you've ever had - but, you do need to reach for a thought that gives a little more breathing space, that is just a little higher up the ladder of emotions. No matter where you want to be, you can get there from here.

13

Stop Tormenting Yourself

God is not the author of fear. You are.

-A Course in Miracles

Remember the old horror movie in which the heroine has been terrorized by a murderous lunatic over the telephone and after having the calls traced is finally told by the police, "Get out! The calls are coming from inside the house!!" Well, there are times when you are just as terrorized by a lunatic and you would do well to remember that these calls are coming from inside the house too – except the house is your own mind. Of course you cannot escape your own mind, but you can change your mind by joining with the Christ Mind.

Today is an ideal day to practice thoughts of peace and surrender to Spirit by giving up worry for one day. Worry is actually using the creative power of the mind to create a future that you do NOT want. This is not God's will for you and is a misuse of the mind's power. It is mental malpractice and though it may not seem like it, with practice and diligence you CAN stop.

Just for today, when any thoughts of fear arise which begin to terrorize you, practice divine surrender by taking 3 deep breaths and affirming Our lesson, "I place the future in the hands of God."

Today you can afford to relax. We are with you as always and right where you are, all things are held perfectly in the hands of God.

14

Your Miracle Escrow Account

No good that you do is ever wasted, even if the intended recipient totally rejects your gift. This is a vibrational Universe and everything that exists exists primarily as a vibration. The good that you choose to do today could even be met with open contempt. But that good goes out as a vibrational force into the ethers and is held in a kind of Miracle Escrow Account until it can be received somewhere by someone – and in the end it is always the giver who gains the greatest benefits. Every act of love increases your own experience of love in the Universe.

What We are reminding you is that worldly results are none of your business. It is your business to fulfill your joyous function as a miracle worker. If you do your part, We assure that God does God's part. You cannot control the receptivity of others and would be foolish to try to keep track of what others let in. Focus instead on what YOU are letting in today and what you are giving out.

Please let Us assure you that We are always watching you, guiding you when you allow it and We have made excellent use of you so often.

The Angels sing songs of gratitude for you every time you act on a loving impulse in even the smallest way. Remember that there is no order of difficulty in miracles, no bigger or smaller. In fact, there are many many miracles that you have performed of which you are totally unaware. People watch you and have been touched by your energy even when you have been so busy that you don't even remember smiling at that person or saying a brief kind word, or making someone laugh in a difficult situation.

When it seems like you are having no positive effect in the world, it is because you are listening to the voice of the ego, unaware of your own rich escrow account. Remember today that every loving thought is an investment that can never be lost or diminished. Every time you bring even the slightest joy or relief to another person, you are spiritually maturing your account.

15

Cultivate Courage

○ ○

You are altogether irreplaceable in the Mind of God. No one else can fill your part in it, and while you leave your part of it empty your eternal place waits for your return . . . you cannot replace the Kingdom and you cannot replace yourself.

-A Course in Miracles

Miracle worker, We encourage you to let your freak flag fly. This requires the consistent development of courage because of the ego's constant desire and yearning to be accepted by other egos. You are domesticated and brain-washed from birth to believe that dampening your natural self is the way to happiness and success. This is why miracles are not a doing but an undoing. Miracles seemingly reunite you with the Self that God created instead of the false one that you were trained to make of yourself.

Do not judge your role in God's plan - remember that there is no big or small in it. God's plan is a plan for your joy and peace and the only sacrifice asked is the sacrifice of giving up fear. The role you play in God's plan is the one in which you experience joy - it is really that simple. When you are joyful, you are IN the Kingdom and are fulfilling your role. Do not tie that role to money a career or worldly success or you will suffer. Your role may have nothing to do with your "work" in the world, or it may, but that is none of your concern. Your part in the plan is achieved whenever you are joyful, even if you are at home alone "doing nothing." We know how to make good use of you without your judgment and interference, but you must relax and trust that God's plan works - yours usually doesn't.

Your role is to be YOU as joyfully as is possible. Your role is to savor being YOU. The world will not be saved by fearful people who are trying to fix it. It will be saved by joyous peaceful happy people. And it take tremendous courage to be your joyful self - without explanation, without guilt, without even earning it. It takes courage to ALLOW your life to be blessed even when you don't "deserve" it; to accept that Divine Grace is yours the moment that you accept it.

16

Listen, Learn and DO

o o o o o o o o o o o o o o o o o o o o o o o o o o o o o o

It is not by trusting yourself that you will gain confidence. But the strength of God in you is successful in all things.

-A Course in Miracles

Confidence and conviction come from doing, not the other way around. Perhaps you think that if you had less fear and more confidence you would try more things and accomplish more good. This is the kind of backward thinking the ego promotes in order to paralyze you. The reverse is true. Confidence comes from DOing - it is built action upon action as you go. Timidness in the miracle worker must be overcome one thought and action at a time.

But miracles themselves are a means of saving time and the "celestial speedup" can move you along in this process quite rapidly if you are willing place your faith in the Light within you rather than in your own personality. To force a fearful personality to take action will only create more stress and inner-conflict. Nor are we encouraging you to become pushy and obnoxious to cover over your terror. This is the opposite of our goal. Real confidence manifests primarily as an outgoing friendliness. Divine confidence is not about forcing or pushing but it is about remembering that within you there is a Strength, a magnetic Force, a dynamic Action which is Divine Intelligence Itself.

Reading, contemplation, deep inner-listening and careful study are extremely important practices for the miracle worker, but remember that "faith without works is dead" is still true today. It begins by simply showing up. If you are not showing up somewhere that you would like to be it is almost always because of lack of confidence caused by some terrifying story you are telling yourself. Instead, tell a new story that you are simply showing up because you were sent by the Cosmic Council of Light to take a step forward into your divine destiny - and what happens after that is none of your business.

17

Stop Arguing For Your Limitations

o o o o o o o o o o o o o o o o o o o o o o o o o o o o o o o

We will not let the beliefs of the world tell us that what God would have us do is impossible. Instead, we will try to recognize that only what God would have us do is possible.

-A Course in Miracles

A miracle worker is simply one who invokes the vibrations of love rather than the illusions of fear in a situation. For the miracle worker, each day is devoted to miracles, which are the shifts in perception from limitation to limitlessness, from facts to possibilities, from anger to peace. The miracle worker does not control conditions but rather influences them with her intentions, thoughts and actions. One cannot force the Qi or really even manipulate it, but it can be worked with, influenced, and even directed. Attempts to manipulate it are misguided miracle impulses. Working with energy is not some strange mystical realm for ascetics alone - everyone is doing it all the time. The point is to learn to do it consciously.

What this requires is an open mind - and an open mind is an open heart. Dear miracle worker, be glad that it is not up to you to accomplish anything here. It is your task to allow the Christ Consciousness to accomplish it through you. Therefore, you can relax. This is not a relaxation akin to sleep for you still remain alert and aware of the current energy vibration. You do not try to push the river or go against the current. It is not necessary to MAKE anything happen. But it is necessary to begin to drop your limiting beliefs about what is possible.

Let Us assure you that past precedent has NOTHING to do with what We will accomplish through you as you begin to tune into the Divine Presence working through you. Begin to cultivate a witnessing consciousness. In fact, it would be very helpful to you to begin a journal in which you record the daily evidence that Divine Love is making itself known in your life more than ever before. Let Us blow your mind.

18

The Wisdom of Penguin Steps

o o o o o o o o o o o o o o o o o o o o o o o o o o o o o o o

Only infinite patience produces immediate results.

-A Course in Miracles

The modern miracle worker would do well to take a lesson from the penguins. Can you imagine just how small one penguin step forward is, how little progress is made and what patience it takes to inch across Antarctica? Think of how impatient you have been in your own journey at times when you have been making strides far larger than a penguin step. Dissatisfaction and impatience are constant themes of the ego because self-criticism helps to keep the ego thought system in power. Ego loves to boast of "multi-tasking" as if it is a good thing. But usually a busy mind is a fearful mind.

Many of you would agree with writer Carrie Fisher who says, "instant gratification takes too long." And this comes back again to the basic problem of the ego mind - constant judgment of the journey and the self. The mind that is preoccupied and busy with constant evaluations has pushed peace and love into a dark corner to be experienced "later." But there is no later. There is only now. Each penguin step forward is happening in the ever-present now. The penguin journey is a success simply because they do not stop or give up just because the going is so slow.

Today you can remember that it is love that moves the penguins forward, not ambition. The inner-desire to bring forth a new creation, in this case a baby penguin, pulls them forward on their slow-moving methodical journey. We invite you to give up self-criticism and judgments today and celebrate each slow step forward in love. The day We want to co-create with you today cannot be mentally evaluated or rushed - it is invoked rather than accomplished. Practice unconditional friendliness toward yourself today as you acknowledge yourself for every tiny step forward.

19

What Will You Make of It?

For many years teacher Louise L. Hay held weekly meetings for hundreds of people facing so-called "terminal" illnesses - and she always began with these very powerful words, "We aren't here to play 'ain't it awful.' We are here to take a positive approach." Friend, you would do well to say the very same thing to yourself as you begin each and every day.

Mental attitudes are habits and the negative fearful ones quickly become mental addictions if they go unchecked. We have noticed that those with these kinds of thought addictions seek out bad news each day on TV, radio, newspapers and even in casual conversation in order to have as many depressing fear-inducing "facts" as possible. For those, We strongly suggest a 30 day news-fast. Cold turkey detox is usually the best way to break the addiction. And during that time it is very important to have support by actively seeking out the good in every situation that arises in thought. This requires patient practice.

The real issue is not what happens to you in this life. The issue is that once something has happened, what will you make of it? You can play "ain't it awful" or you can move into a deeper faith as you begin gathering up any tiny scrap of evidence that feeds your optimism and inner-peace. In time you can become someone who becomes addicted to loving joyful thoughts. Remember, though Pollyanna was a fictional character, she was a major archetype of the kind of miracle workers We are busy training.

"Miracles are habits . . . Miracles are everyone's right, but purification is necessary first."

-A Course in Miracles

20

Call Off The Search

Yet the ego, though encouraging the search for love very actively, makes one proviso: do not find it. Its dictates, then, can be summed up simply as: "Seek and do NOT find."

-A Course in Miracles

Call off the search. Just for one day. Take the day off from all yearning, striving, struggling and seeking of any kind.

Whether your search for "love" is your search for a romantic partner, worldly success, approval, understanding, acceptance, healing, money, security, a "better" body, the right spiritual path or even more bliss . . . just let it go . . . just for one day. Call in the bloodhounds and make peace with your life just the way it is and just the way it is not. Just for today.

Whatever you do today do it for the simple pleasure of the doing . . . without trying to get anything or get anywhere. Simply show up without your usual agenda and be open to what comes. Miracle workers have been sent out quite effectively without "purse, nor scrip" and found themselves lacking nothing. But you'll never know for yourself until you begin to practice these days of trusting.

Tomorrow you can go right back to your frantic searching if you like. But for now - Slow Down, Breathe, Relax, Let Go.

21

Hey, I Just Work Here

o o o o o o o o o o o o o o o o o o o o o o o o o o o o o o o o

All that must be recognized, however, is that birth is not the beginning, and death is not the end.

-A Course in Miracles

It is good to remember that physical incarnation is a temp job; an assignment to be completed and to be enjoyed. And when this assignment is over, there will be more to enjoy. Earth is not the only school in the Universe, and though We encourage you to fully inhabit the role you play, try not to get so attached and territorial - even about your body. Nothing here is ever yours - it's all provided as part of the assignment and you'll leave every bit of "stuff" behind for your replacements, including your body. Everything gets recycled and nothing is ever truly wasted. We have observed that the less attached you are to your particular storyline, the more you tend to enjoy your time here. It is possible and We encourage you to be fully-engaged without being attached. This does take some practice.

Physical death is neither a punishment nor a failure and length of life has nothing to do with how successful the assignment was. Many stay for quite a long time avoiding what they came to do while others have been known to incarnate for only a few hours and have concluded their entire assignment quite neatly. We do not see death as something to be avoided but rather know it to simply be the end of a particular assignment - a kind of graduation actually.

So Our guidance for you is that you enjoy your own death experience as much as possible. Don't make so much of HOW or WHEN it comes. You all walk through a variety of doors - cancer, heart attacks, murder, car accidents, or just the wear and tear of an old well-worn body. It is your constant judgments about the how and when that make of death an enemy. But We assure you that when the time is exactly right and it is time for you to go, the very second you make that final transition you will see death as a warm open door that only leads to MORE life, not less.

22

Mistakes, You've Made a Few

○ ○

The Holy Spirit is not delayed in His teaching by your mistakes.
He can be held back only by your unwillingness to let them go.

-A Course in Miracles

Ruminating on your errors and on where you got it wrong is not the same thing as learning from those mistakes. In fact, it is actually another way to set up the momentum to repeat those same mistakes later on. Guilt is a very attractive and dynamic vibratory energy. The ego gets very excited about anything that increases guilt because it sets up a vicious cycle of suffering, remorse, self-hatred, shame and guilt, exhaustion, suppression and then a repeat of the mistake, which starts the process all over again.

There is another way. Let it all go in sincere surrender to God. To repent means to "turn around" - you're going in the wrong direction. When you sincerely repent from your mistakes, you turn away from the darkness of guilt and shame and turn toward God's Light. This is not a suppression of your mistake - it is an honest accounting of what you did, of your sincere desire to be released from the guilt, of your willingness to make right whatever you can make right, and then the acceptance of forgiveness and grace as you seek wisdom and guidance on learning what there is to learn from the situation.

Once you've gone through this process, do not look back. Stop dragging the dead past into the present. Get right back on the path again. If the GPS system in your car went out and you got lost, hundreds of miles off track and then later the system came back on, there would be no need to explain to it how you got lost, why you got lost, how long you were lost, whose fault it was, etc. No, you would quickly allow the GPS to take over as your guidance system again and no matter how far off-track you'd gotten, you'd be back on the road and making progress as soon as you decide to go forward. It is the same with Us. We will guide you as soon as you are willling to move on.

23

Magnificent Obsession

o o o o o o o o o o o o o o o o o o o o o o o o o o o o o o o o

*I am here only to be truly helpful . . . I am content to be wherever
He wishes, knowing He goes there with me. I will be healed as I
let Him teach me to heal.*

--A Course in Miracles

We are so happy when a miracle worker is busy helping one of our
brothers or sisters. It is one of the few times when We can make
meaningful progress in the life of the miracle worker because she has
finally stopped interfering with the flow of the Tao. Oh how We love
it when you get out of the way! When you are busy being of service to
another you take a break from worry, self-obsession, manipulating and
scheming. It is in those moments that We rush in with all the Healing
that you've been asking for.

So often you ask for help and then keep two tightly closed fists
which simply are unavailable for receiving anything. When you help
others, your hands open up to be used and We can easily bless an open
hand. An open hand is accessible to Grace.

We would write a new song for you called, "What have you done
today to make you feel humble?" Humility is not humiliation - it is a
lack of ego. Try to remember that "pride will not produce miracles."
The more you humble yourself to be a vessel of Light, the more you

will be lifted up. As in the movie, this giving can become a "magnificent obsession" - one that replaces all the old fucked up obsessions. And if you can quietly be of relatively anonymous non-attached service, on a consistent basis, you may look up and find that while you were busy, We solved your problems for you.

This does not mean you should use this as an excuse to not deal with your own personal responsibilities or ignore taking care of yourself while you burn out doing service projects. There is always the yin and the yang, the inflow and the outflow. In your meditations with Us, seek the wisdom to find your own personal balance and We will Help you.

24

A Fenced Yard Is Not Safe

o o o o o o o o o o o o o o o o o o o o o o o o o o o o o o o o o o

In my defenselessness my safety lies.

-A Course in Miracles

Non-resistance and non-contention. Breathe in those words. Let them settle into your cellular structure to become a part of your problem-solving repertoire. The simple Truth is that there is nothing in this world that can protect you when you are entertaining attack thoughts in your own mind. The magnetic laws of the Universe can only reflect back to you what you think and it will seem as though it is being attracted to you - but in actuality, it is YOU who are attracted to it. When attack is activated in you, you will see it everywhere because you are subconsciously drawn to it.

One of you told us a story about how you watched your beloved little canine companion being killed by a coyote who had jumped over the fence and into your back yard, trapping the dog with its murderer in the "safe" space. You said those words to us that day, "a fenced yard is not safe." We are not suggesting you tear down the fence in your yard, but We are suggesting that you tear down the fences from around your heart and mind. Only a defenseless heart is truly safe.

It is true that you create what you defend against. By pushing against something you literally activate it in your life and bring it front and center in your experience. This causes you to build up your armor, your defenses and your strategies. And it is entirely hopeless and exhausting. It is the war within and without. The war on drugs, the war on crime, the war on poverty, the war on sickness, the war on aging - fighting, fighting, fighting - and always losing.

The only way to win is to stop the war today - in your own thoughts. Where are you at war in your life? If you are against something, you are at war. Many are at war with their own bodies and think attack thoughts against them all day long. You may want to start there. Make peace with your body or whatever else you are at war with. Drop the sword and the shield and relax - be FOR something and against nothing today.

25

Directing Your Energy

○ ○

Without a clear-cut, positive goal, set at the outset, the situation just seems to happen, and makes no sense until it has already happened.

-A Course in Miracles

Perhaps you are familiar with the phrase "act as if" which so many new thought students love to say. But the question which follows that is . . . how? HOW does one act as if? Our answer is to play the lunch game.

The lunch game is played most effectively with just one other person and can be done over lunch, dinner, breakfast, coffee and even on the telephone if necessary. It begins by both players moving in consciousness exactly 6 months into the future, no more and no less. This is the PERFECT amount of time in order to shift the vibration for the greatest joy and least amount of stress. Each player "pretends" that it is 6 months from today and then ABSOLUTELY ALL conversation is from the vantage point of that date. For instance, if it is June 19, both players speak from start to finish of their time spent together as if today is December 19, speaking happily and calmly of how wonderfully all things have unfolded over the past 6 months.

The idea is that you begin to LIVE the vibration of 6 months from now when all that currently is an issue has either been entirely resolved or is moving in that direction or the seedlings of new aspects of your life are beginning to sprout. BE VERY UN-SPECIFIC ABOUT HOW IT IS RESOLVED OR IS RESOLVING. This is also a great opportunity to begin to sow seeds for what you are calling into your life next. Your part is not to TELL the Universe HOW it is done - your part is the WHAT. Make this believable and not huge. The bigger the leap from where you are, the less effective the game will be. Don't go from living in a studio apartment to owning a house. Don't go from weighing 300 pounds to weighing 150 pounds. Make it the next logical unfolding from where you currently stand, not something AMAZING. Be somewhat vague because the point is to get into the FEELING that everything is moving forward in a smooth and satisfactory way.

And do not include ANYONE ELSE or their journey. This is NOT the time to vision for your husband, children or anyone else - they have their own path and free will. This is ONLY about you and your vibrational journey. You may envision YOUR experience and feelings toward them, but not what happens for them. Stay in your own business. Make it light. Make it fun. Make it somewhat vague as far as the HOW anything happened. That is none of your business. Your vibration is your business.

As you shift your vibration, the outer world cannot help but reflect the inner. But most importantly, you will have shifted from worry to joy in your now. We STRONGLY urge you to do this once a month and keep a written log of the results over the next year.

26

You Don't Live the Life You Deserve, You Live the Life You THINK You Deserve

o o o o o o o o o o o o o o o o o o o o o o o o o o o o o

My grace is sufficient for thee: for My strength is made perfect in weakness.

-II Corinthians 12:9

Grace is the undeserved favor of the Universe. It flows equally over the "just and the unjust" alike. It is like water - it flows freely from on high and goes downward to the lowly places filling every opening equally. And where there is no opening It flows right over it and cannot enter. It cannot be earned or achieved but it does require a willingness to let It in.

Have you noticed how those who work the hardest on your planet often have the least when clearly they "deserve" the most? This is merely a matter of ignorance - they do not know because they have not been taught. And you must have also noticed how many who seem to contribute nothing of any real value have cups that runneth over. It is only because they have allowed it in - in fact, they actually EXPECT the good to come rushing into their lives.

Now, this has nothing to do with happiness or joy - those who have little are in fact often as happy or happier than those who have many more material blessings but We are merely speaking here in terms of the expansion of your willingness to receive. The lesson is that regardless of your perceived limitations, weaknesses, character defects, past experience or what you deserve and have worked for - the great Mother Tao is only limited by what you are willing to let in today. Again, do not argue for your limitations or they will be yours.

27

Changing Hearts

○ ○

He heals the broken in heart, and binds up their wounds.

-Psalm 147:3

"People don't change" is a terrible affirmation that many people use to try to guard their hearts from yet another disappointment. But the real pain comes from wanting people to be different than they are and from having expectations for them to meet. Spiritual maturing is about releasing people to be whoever they are - even if you don't approve or like it.

The simple truth is that there is no way to NOT change in the physical universe. Everyone is changing and changing all the time. All are moving in one direction or another. Your basic personality may never change but it is moving in one direction or the other. You are either becoming softer, more open and expansive within that personality or you are becoming more rigid, harder and more contracted. The choice is: better or bitter?

This is what heart break does to people - it shatters the heart and the person goes in the direction of fear and bitterness or it breaks the heart open and the person goes toward a deeper love and a more compassionate understanding of life.

This is your choice today - better or bitter?

28

Birthing or Building

Jesus said, 'If you bring forth what is within you, what you bring forth will save you. If you do not bring forth what is within you, what you do not bring forth will destroy you.'

-The Gospel of Thomas

There are two main aspects to life and living; love and the law.

Building is an external action-oriented happening - it is the realm of the dynamic laws of the Universe. When you live by the laws of the Universe you are in a legalistic cause and effect realm of action and reaction. This puts the human mind in control rather than Divine Mind and so it is based on the highest level of thinking of which the ego is capable. It is necessary as part of your growth to learn to use the laws so that you do not live in a victim consciousness. Still, at this level, law of attraction can only go as far as your own little intellect will allow. Spiritual maturity demands that you ascend higher than living by law.

Birthing is something else altogether. It is an inner-movement and is a much higher vibrational experience than building because it is true co-creation at its best. It is not based on what you know or can see. It is not based on what you want or think you need - it is the result of putting love at the center of your life. Because it is an inner-experience you cannot control it any more than a pregnant woman can control what is happening in the womb. What is happening is the result of a willingness to allow the Divine Urge to create THROUGH you rather than BY you. This is the true goal of physical incarnation - it is why you came here - not to GET something, but to be a vessel for the Light to come through. Building takes effort. Birthing requires allowing.

Just for today, let go of what you are trying to accomplish and build. Something wonderful is wanting to be born through you, today and every day. Your job is to relax and enjoy the process. And what you bring forth will not only be a gift to the world, it will be a gift for you.

29

Making Friends With It

○ ○

No longer is the world our enemy, for we have chosen that we be its friend.

-A Course in Miracles

Whatever is going on in your life today, you have the choice to make of it a friend or an enemy. When you make an enemy, you are at war. This internal war causes resistance, fear, attack thoughts, strategic thinking and a loss of self.

There is nothing you cannot make friends with if you are willing to let your mind be healed of judgment and opinions. Relax your mind for a moment. Just for a few moments KNOW that there is nothing to get, nothing to fix, nothing to change - there is no thought to hold on to, no thought to push away and there is nothing to get rid of - just a gentle opening to receive the blessings of the day.

Stop the war today and make friends with whatever comes along. Be a peacemaker and be blessed. Just for today, remind yourself frequently, "There is nothing for me to do but receive."

30

The Better It Gets, The Better It Gets

○ ○

Our exercises for today will be happy ones, in which we offer thanks for the passing of the old and the beginning of the new.

-A Course in Miracles

This is a day for savoring. Savor the golden moments today. They are there if you ask for them and are willing to see them. Take your time as much as possible. Make a conscious effort to be a gracious receiver of the gifts of God by enjoying all that has been given. Look around your world and focus on the things that stimulate appreciation and joy in you.

The more that you become an awakened appreciator, savoring the good that is given, the more the good will flood every aspect of your being and your life. This is only the beginning.

31

Post a Guard

o o o o o o o o o o o o o o o o o o o o o o o o o o o o o o o

I cannot let you leave your mind unguarded, or you will not be able to help me. Miracle working entails a full realization of the power of thought in order to avoid miscreation.

-A Course in Miracles

Your early metaphysicians told their students to "post a guard at the door of your mind" and this is perhaps even more important now than it was then. It is so easy for you to become over-stimulated by all the fearful information you allow into your mind. The mind is the source of creation and whatever you allow into it and believe will begin to affect you in many ways.

"Garbage in, garbage out" is not only true for computers, it is true for the ultimate computer, which is your own mind. No one else is thinking in your mind and no one else can take your emotional journey for you. You have Divine Guidance and Help, but never at the expense of your own free will. What you think is ultimately up to you and you can become aware of your thoughts by the way you feel. Use this to your advantage. When you do not like the way you are feeling, begin to question the thoughts that you have allowed into your mind - they are the source. Then, clean up your vibration by sweeping those thoughts away as you would sweep the dust from your front porch. You allowed them in, now they are being swept back out. You may say that you have no control over the fearful thoughts that you ruminate on, but if a tooth fell out of your mouth everytime you had one, you would find that you could stop it very quickly. Fear is a habit.

Do not be lazy about this, particularly in the beginning. Be mindful of the things you are reading, the conversations you are involved in, the TV shows that you watch. They are wallpapering your mind. Be vigilant for focusing your thoughts in the direction of the Christ Mind first thing in the morning by setting an intention for how you want to FEEL that day, then invite Spirit to allow in only the thoughts that will support those feelings. Peaceful people think peaceful thoughts even in the midst of a chaotic day. Loving people think loving thoughts even in the midst of unloving situations. This takes practice. Be gentle but firm with yourself and We will begin to guide you to the happiness you deserve.

32

Keep It Simple

o o o o o o o o o o o o o o o o o o o o o o o o o o o o o o o o o o

When your learning promotes depression instead of joy, you cannot be listening to God's joyous Teacher and learning His lessons.

-A Course in Miracles

Many wonder how they can tell the difference between the voice of the ego and the Voice for God. It is really quite simple and your emotional guidance system will let you know. When you feel peace or joy, you are listening to God's joyous Teacher. When you feel worry, fear, anger, depression - basically anything that does not feel good, you are believing the ego's thought system.

Joy and excitement are not the same thing. Excitement is often the result of the ego thinking it is going to "get" what it wants. Joy is a state of being which may have nothing to do with the circumstances of your life. The ego will try to get you excited and it is always about the future and what you may GET. This is how it robs you of the peace of the present moment. It is wonderful to have an optimistic outlook on the future and even to have things to look forward to, but if it whips you into excitement, you are starting to leave the God Zone.

If what you are thinking brings you peace in your present - that is God. If what you are thinking brings you joy in your present - that is God. There is no need to make it any more complicated than that. You can check in with yourself throughout the day with that simple little test - am I feeling peace and joy in this moment? That's how you will know if you are in the God Zone or not. When you get lost, just reach for the closest downstream non-resistant thought and you are on your way back home again.

33

Being the Change

Any attempt you make to correct a brother means that you believe correction by you is possible and this can only be the arrogance of the ego.

-A Course in Miracles

We cannot help but notice how many angry people drive around with bumper stickers which read, "Be the change you want to see in the world." It is often not so much an affirmation as an instruction to others, "YOU be the change that I want to see in the world."

Remember that "to teach is to demonstrate." It is not possible to give what you do not have. To try to teach peace while harboring anger, resentments, judgment, guilt and blame is a waste of time. Do your best to stay in your own yard, little miracle worker. It is your energy, your vibration, which teaches most powerfully and effectively - much much more than your words and preaching.

When you are focused on where someone else is getting it wrong, you have already exiled yourself from the Kingdom and cannot be of real help to anyone. Instead, ask for Help in changing your own mind about the other - release them and relinquish the evidence you have gathered against them. Yes, We want you to help each other, but in a non-attached, non-judgmental way. When you can communicate without judgment and without attachment, there is a much greater chance that you will actually be demonstrating what you desire to teach. What do you choose to demonstrate today?

34

The Divine Harvest

o o o o o o o o o o o o o o o o o o o o o o o o o o o o o o o

Only what you have not given can be lacking in any situation.

-A Course in Miracles

There are two major patterns when it comes to energy. There is stagnation and there is circulation. Energy is either moving and flowing freely in and out, in and out - or the channels are being slowed down and the energy is pooling, staying separate and shut off from the greater flow.

When people become fearful, the first thing they usually do is stop circulating their energy freely. In other words, they stop giving. Once the giving stops, the inflow automatically stops too. What you withhold is always withheld from you because the Universal mirror only reflects you back to you. And the more afraid you get, the more you withhold and the more you withhold, the more you are depleted.

When living under the magnetic laws of the Universe you sow exactly what you reap - exactly. If you love roses, do not get busy planting apple trees. In planting, you give to the earth the exact thing that you want to harvest. This is true in every area of the world. If you plant love, you will reap a love harvest. If you plant service, you will reap a harvest of service. The exact thing that you give, is the exact thing that will come back to you. Without active constant sowing, there is no active constant harvesting.

The only difference between the energetic world and the farm is that your harvest often does not come from the same location where you planted. You may give enormous amounts of unconditional love to Bob, but Bob still decides to leave you. Nevertheless, your love harvest is guaranteed by the Universe. Check with your dog - animals never withhold your harvest from you. In other words, do not decide the people or situations by which your blessings will come - that is none of your business. Once you have planted, your job is to simply be open to the blessings that come and NOT to determine the who and where.

35

Fuck Forgiveness

o o o o o o o o o o o o o o o o o o o o o o o o o o o o o o o o o o o

Forgiveness is a selective remembering.

-A Course in Miracles

We got your attention with that one didn't We? Sometimes a good shock to the miracle worker's system is necessary in order to get you to let go of an old stale paradigm. Forgiveness is just such a paradigm. The ego's idea of forgiveness is so perverted and distorted that it makes true forgiveness nearly impossible for most humans. It is a "forgiveness to destroy" in which there is still a wounded party and a guilty party. Within that realm there is no unity, only separation and guilt.

We are suggesting that you replace the word "forgive" with the words "let go." That's all it really means anyhow. To forgive is to let go. Let go of the file of evidence. Shred the files that prove guilt. Stop trying to prove the case for the prosecution.

We are not talking about suppressing or pushing feelings down or pretending. But We are talking about total release from the story altogether. This is only possible when you are willing to let it go. HOW to let it go? Stop picking it up every day. There is no how in letting go, there is only a how in holding on. When you stop the mental action of holding on, you've automatically let go. Children do it when they are too exhausted to cling onto their toy any longer and they finally fall into sleep. Aren't you at least that tired by now?

So We say "fuck forgiveness, let go instead." Practice it for a while. Say to yourself and others, "Oh, I've let that go. I've released that. I've surrendered that story. I'm not picking that up anymore." You WILL shift your vibration and experience the freedom you seek. One powerful way to let go is through the work of Byron Katie: www.thework.com

36

Controlling the Universe

o o o o o o o o o o o o o o o o o o o o o o o o o o o o o o o o o

You who cannot even control yourself should hardly aspire to control the Universe.

-A Course in Miracles

Set them all free today miracle worker. You know the ones We mean - all those whose minds you would like to influence and control. Free will means that everyone gets to choose what they will think and how they will perceive. Your efforts to try to control their minds and actions and opinions is the cause of the majority of your suffering.

People like you or they don't. People love you or they don't. People approve of you or they don't. And none of it is any of your business because though they may have a story about you, all stories are all projections of the self.

So when we say "set them free" what really happens is that you set yourself free. When you learn to live without controlling, strategizing and manipulating the minds, opinions and approval of others, you will walk through the world with a buoyancy and a peace that truly passes all understanding. You may think you NEED their approval because they are your spouse or your employer or your abuser or your audience, but this only means that you have confused them with your Source and since no human being can be that, you have ultimately made them your jailer because you've imprisoned yourself with what THEY think of you.

Call back your power. Call back your Spirit. Realign with your Source and set everyone else free. They already are anyhow so you might as well get on board with reality and enjoy the ride!

37

Right Action

o o o o o o o o o o o o o o o o o o o o o o o o o o o o o o o o o

*Let us therefore be determined to remember what we want today,
that we may unify our thoughts and actions meaningfully, and
achieve only what God would have us do this day.*

-A Course in Miracles

It is so satisfying to take an inspired action which moves you in the
direction you want to go. We speak here so much about getting out of
the way and "allowing" that you may think that action is not a part of
the process, but faith without action is dead. After all, Our motto is
"listen, learn and DO."

Our point is that it is not the action which really accomplishes
the desired end or that is truly creative. Everything is vibrational in
this Universe and it is only on that level than anything meaningful
is ever accomplished. However, action is one of the primary ways
that vibration is shifted. The "lunch game" is an action that shifts
vibration. Meditation is an action which shifts vibration. Exercise is an
act which shifts vibration. They are so closely tied that it may LOOK
like the action is what created the end result - but it was not, it was the
vibrational shift.

If the action does NOT shift the vibration, results will either not
come at all, or they will not be sustained for long. You see this all the

time with people who yo-yo in the various areas of their lives. They are taking actions which temporarily shift their vibration but then they revert to the old vibe at some point. Our concern is that you let go of your egoic preoccupation with the endless "what should I DO" question. Instead, try asking your Inner-Being "What is the best vibration to get into about this and how can I best move into that vibration?" Then when the answer comes, know that this is the right action to shift YOUR vibration at this time - it may not work for anyone else and it may not even work for you at a different time or in a different situation. Remember that this is a highly individualized curriculum and not a one-size-fits-all path.

Taking action is often the very best way to lift yourself out of old stuck-feeling patterns and habitual ruts you sometimes get into because action can be a tremendous stimulator of new thoughts and thought creates vibration - all working together for good.

38

Today's Prayer

Dear God,

I assume You're in control here.

I'll be very interested to see how

You work this one out.

If you need me,

You know where to find me.

Thanks so much!

Amen

39

Not Now, Right Now

○ ○

Babies scream in rage if you take away a knife or scissors, although they may well harm themselves if you do not. In this sense you are still a baby. You have no sense of real self-preservation, and are likely to decide that you need precisely what would hurt you most.

-A Course in Miracles

We want very much to gently mentor you to spiritual maturity because of the great joy and freedom that it will give you. But this is a process of undoing and takes patience and tremendous willingness on your part. Old concepts, fantasies and attachments gradually and sometimes not so gradually begin to reveal themselves as tinsel and shabby substitutes for your real treasure and this often enrages the ego along the way.

We understand that you want what you want and of course that you want it yesterday. The temptations of this world are extremely powerful for an unguarded and spiritually immature mind. This tendency to indulge rather than nourish yourself can be very problematic. The immature mind wants the "thing" that will give it sensory satisfaction in the now, even if the price down the road is very steep. The mature mind has a diamond in its pocket and is therefore not impoverished in the now even when forgoing immediate gratification.

If you are willing to relax your grip and your desire to control, We will give you your true heart's desire and not just what the insatiable hungry monkey mind demands. You can forever live in a future-oriented mindset of trying to get what you want, or you can shift into appreciating what you already have which puts you in the peace of the present moment.

We encourage you to tell us what you want in as joyful and high a vibration as possible - then, surrender it and let it go to Us to handle. We'll sift through it all and return to you the very best content possible, perhaps not in the form you expected but definitely in the form that will serve you best over the long run.

40

Twenty- One Penguin Steps Forward

o o o o o o o o o o o o o o o o o o o o o o o o o o o o o o o o o o

This is the time for faith. You let this goal be set for you. That was an act of faith. Do not abandon faith now that the rewards of faith are being introduced.

-A Course in Miracles

Usually there are so many things that you want to change about yourself or your life that you tend to overwhelm yourself, resulting in either paralysis or intense driven stress from trying to motivate yourself into a BIG change. This is not God's will for you. There is another way - the water-course way of gentle consistent change over a period of time. Water can wear away a mountain over time and your daily consistent efforts can wear away old fearful habits too.

Do you realize that in just 21 days you can gently develop a positive new habit? We suggest that you pick just one or perhaps two things - very small positive changes that will not overwhelm you. You might want to add a 15 minute walk to your day. Or you could choose to spend 21 days praising as many people a day as you can. Even adding 5 minutes of morning meditation for 21 days will shift you to a new vibrational frequency in a way that is gentle and simple.

If you start today, in 21 days you WILL see progress. Be kind to yourself and give up perfectionism. Just practice "showing up" for yourself in this way for these 3 weeks and give yourself credit for every step forward and instant forgiveness for every stumble or mis-step. We are with you. We will Help you if you are merely willing to take those little daily penguin steps forward.

41

Today's Metaphysical Prescription:

Spend as much time as possible in "the Miracle Zone" today. The Zone is a place where thinking, reasoning and trying to figure things out simply does not work. To get into the Zone you leave behind all the "mental/spiritual techniques" that you've mastered and simply lose yourself in the dance. The Zone is beyond techniques - beyond words and even thoughts. Here is Our prescription for getting in the Zone. Once you are there, you won't even need to do this.

• Less asking for, more allowing

• Less wanting, more appreciating

• Less fixing what's wrong, more savoring what's right

• Less intending, more accepting

42

Backsliding

You who have tried to throw yourself away and valued God so little, hear me speak for Him and for yourself. You cannot understand how much your Father loves you, for there is no parallel in your experience of the world to help you understand it.

-A Course in Miracles

Little miracle worker, of course you are going to have times where it seems like you are backsliding on your path. You will be happily moving forward in love and fearlessness for a time and then perhaps one little thing will throw your joyful concentration toward your personal darkness again. SLIPPING UP IS PART OF THE LEARNING CURVE - DO NOT LET THIS DETER YOU. Do not indulge the tendency toward guilt and punishment.

Too often you allow your mind to use your errors and missteps as an excuse to cut yourself off from Source when it is Source that IS the correcting agent. God does not care that you are naked and embarrassed so DO NOT HIDE. Bring your mistakes to the Light and they will be gently released and you will be set right back on your path in an instant. Do not continue to ring the bell of the mistake - simply ask with sincerity that your thinking be corrected in your present moment Divine Love will restore you the moment you are willing to be restored. Too many of you have the tendency to delay your progress after a "slip" by thinking that you have to punish yourself for a while and earn grace again. GRACE CANNOT BE EARNED OR IT IS NOT GRACE!

Every prodigal daughter and son is instantly restored to the Kingdom without punishment when they return to the Higher Path. When you slide back into an old pattern do not throw in the towel - raise the white flag of surrender and accept God's Grace as you step right back onto the Path of Light again.

43

Cast Your Cares

o o o o o o o o o o o o o o o o o o o o o o o o o o o o o o o

Do you really believe you can plan for your safety and joy better than He can? You need be neither careful nor careless; you need merely cast your cares upon Him because He careth for you. You are His care because He loves you.

-A Course in Miracles

When you are afraid it is because you have forgotten Who you are and have believed yourself to be separate from your Source again. Ask yourself, if you feel separate from God, who moved? If fish were able to think as you do, one of them might feel separate from the ocean while swimming around because the ocean is so pervasively everywhere that it would see no evidence of the ocean. The reality is that the ocean has not moved or gone away anymore than your Divine Source could leave you.

But if you have allowed your thinking to lead you away from awareness of this Divine Force, you will feel abandoned and begin worrying about your future. The mind will start planning, scheming and strategizing - and not from joy and inspiration, but from belief in limitation, lack and finite resources.

Our brother Jesus said, "Consider the birds of the air: for they sow not, neither do they reap, nor gather into barns; yet your heavenly

Father feeds them. Are you not much better than they?" The major difference is that they do not worry, and they do not disconnect their awareness of Source. They are so connected that they all know the exact day, hour and minute to migrate for the winter - all without a "to do" list or a brain-storming meeting. They stay connected and Guidance tells them what to do, when and how to do it.

You need be neither careful nor careless in your daily life - just stay connected to your Source and all that you need will be yours. Do you really think the Universe has a plan for you that doesn't work?

44

Praying for Results

○ ○

Prayer is the medium of miracles.

-A Course in Miracles

The least effective form of prayer is petitionary prayer which asks for specific outcomes. It certainly does not bring you the peace that you deserve and it is an egoic spiritually immature form. It's not that far removed from wishing or relying on "luck" and superstitious talismans. It's not "bad" - it's simply quite low on the evolutionary scale.

In petitionary prayer you want God to get in alignment with your plans and strategies. In true prayer you align yourself with the Divinely unfolding Universe. It is a kind of peaceful surrender of your way to THE way. This DOES produce the peace that you deserve as it moves you back into alignment with your Source instead of trying to bring Source into your nightmare.

Mother Father God, Here I am. Show me Your love! I give this situation and my thoughts about it to You now. I surrender my plans and my life to You today. Today I seek and find Your peace as I release everyone and everything to Your perfect wisdom, power and Grace. Heal my mind and restore my heart. And if You can make good use of me today, I am Yours. I know that as I go where you instruct and do Your will, You will be taking care of my problems for me and guiding me in all the right ways. Thank You for this day of peaceful release. I love You.

45

You Cannot Outgive God

○ ○

You cannot even give a blessing in perfect gentleness. Would you know of One Who gives forever, and Who knows of nothing except giving?

-A Course in Miracles

It is true that you can never outgive God, but it can be a very enjoyable past-time to try. This is a game that you can never ever win because this account is forever out of balance with the surplus always in your favor. Even every breath is given to you freely. It's true that there is a reciprocal relationship between you and the plant world with your breath, but this is hardly the result of your personal effort or generous nature.

No this is not the human nature. Yet your true nature IS one of unending generosity and givingness because you are so like your Creator. You have learned scarcity here and it is unnatural to you. Now is the time to unlearn all that you have learned here that has not brought you peace. In time you will learn to hold nothing back and will not even want anything that you cannot give away freely. This is the complete reversal of all that this world has tried to teach you.

Nothing is so full of the vibration of impoverishment than endless acquisition. The desire and bargaining for love is the very thing that blocks the experience. The hungry ghosts can never be satisfied and the only way to exorcise them is to begin giving away the very thing that you want. It is through the giving that you will begin to understand what it means to say that you cannot outgive God. This is not "giving to get" and it is not a "getting rid of" out of guilt. You may make those mistakes in the beginning, but it will not last. Ultimately you will give as a statement of Who you are, having nothing whatsoever to do with the things of this world. When you forget who you are and feel lacking and impoverished, give first and you will begin to remember your Self again - and in that very moment your cup will be running over.

46

Resisting Peace

o o o o o o o o o o o o o o o o o o o o o o o o o o o o o o o

The first obstacle that peace must flow across is your desire to get rid of it.

-A Course in Miracles

Be careful of the tendency of the mind to become addicted to solving problems. The fixation on fixing rather than on appreciating is a kind of mental bondage.

How much of your day is spent trying to solve problems and "improve" people and situations and self? Do you really think this is what reality is for? The ego itself is a kind of mental fixation and ego loves nothing more than to continue creating the concept of "problems" which are incapable of being solved.

Some of you become so good at "trouble-shooting" and fixing things that you feel useless if there is not a problem in front of you so you manufacture trouble where there is none. This is a waste of your true Creative talents and a delay of the miracle that would heal the mind.

Begin to make friends with peace today. Begin by simply shifting your focus to what is good and true and beautiful in your world, in your life. You'll be happily surprised at how many so-called problems begin to vanish when you take your attention away from fixing and put it on the simple pleasures of life that already surround you every day.

47

Is That The Hill You Want to Die On?

○ ○
Do you prefer that you be right or happy?

-A Course in Miracles

It is almost tragic to notice how often many of you argue FOR something that actually makes you feel much much worse - how you argue for some limitation that you don't even WANT to be true - how often you fight a battle which is going to feel horrible even if you "win" it. Haven't you ever noticed that when you are in that defensive state that even when someone tries to offer a solution or another way of thinking you simply argue that they are wrong, insensitive and simply do not understand the depths and complications of your particular unique and special problem? The ego is endlessly contentious and loves to fight, but more than anything it is easily offended.

We are suggesting that you choose to never be offended again - that you give up the tendency to go into battle. Waving the white flag in this case is not an act of cowardice but an act of faith. It may begin slowly by becoming wiser about "choosing your battles" as you begin to relax old knee-jerk reactions to having your buttons pushed. This is very good. It is the miraculous expansion of time between stimulus and response and this small expansion can be enough time to actually CHOOSE a response rather than simply REACT.

It begins with awareness and then practice. Practice expanding the gap between stimulus and response. Between the time something is said to you and the time you respond, look to see if you are coming from a truly open and defenseless place. If you are not, then you are about to enter the battle again and if this is the case, take an extra moment to ask yourself, "Is this the hill I want to die on?" In other words, am I going to allow this to be the thing that kills my peace of mind and murders my joy today?

48

Fuck Meditation

o o o o o o o o o o o o o o o o o o o o o o o o o o o o o o o o o o

And if you find resistance strong and dedication weak, you are not ready. Do not fight yourself.

-A Course in Miracles

Meditation is another one of those words that has been so over used and misused that you're better off without it. It has all kinds of "should" connotations on it and pseudo-mystical underpinnings which are simply not helpful.

Instead, simply sit and practice stillness for a few minutes every day - the morning is the very best time of all but ANY time is good enough and will be very beneficial. Open your mind to God and ask for the Divine Presence to fill your mind as you relax and breathe, relax and breathe. Let your mind grow quiet and allow your heart to soften. Try to sit for 5 minutes or so each day for 21 consecutive days just as a little game in which there is no winning or losing. Do this for fun, not to achieve anything. You are not trying to get anywhere or to be "good" at this or to experience some altered state of mind.

In reality, stress and worry are your altered states for they are unnatural. A quiet spacious mind is the return to your natural state. So simply practice this quiet mind technique each day for 21 days and take note of the effects it has on the unfolding peace of your days and nights. Don't wait. Start today. The 5 minutes before you are the perfect ones to start with - We are with you in this and will help you if you will just make the slightest effort.

49

Not Two Powers

° °

The opposite of love is fear, but what is all encompassing can have no opposite. This course can therefore be summed up very simply in this way: Nothing real can be threatened. Nothing unreal exists. Herein lies the peace of God.

-A Course in Miracles

It is the belief in two powers that causes all the conflict in your world - both the inner and outer. Your early metaphysicians stressed this over and over and over again. Somewhere along the way it got lost and the belief in two powers crept into metaphysics and has reinforced the illusory split in the minds of the children of God.

There is no darkness, no fear, no devil, no source of sickness or pain or poverty - these are all aspects of maya, the great illusion. Even the ego We speak of is non-existent and is only a word used to describe a thought system based on the belief in separation. To believe in two powers is to begin the battle against one of them. And this simply gives your power to a nightmare and wastes your vital energies. Remember that Brother Jesus said, "resist not evil" because He knew that it was not real and that to resist it would be giving illusions power over your mind.

Whatever issues may confront your mind today, remember that there is only One Power, One Source, One Force in all of the Universe. If you have any problem today it comes from a misguided belief in two powers, one for good and one for bad. Remember this and then simply realign yourself with the One Power - nothing to fight against, nothing to resist, nothing to fix or change or figure out. Just breathe and return to Center. All is well.

50

A Closed Mouth Never Gets Fed

You merely ask the question. The answer is given.

-A Course in Miracles

I wonder if you have any idea how much We love to Help you, to give to you, to send you gifts and encouragement all along your pathway? We see you struggle so needlessly, trying so hard to do it on your own as if you were a little child refusing parental aid while screaming "I CAN DO IT MYSELF!" And since God established free will as yours, We never interfere where We are not invited in.

Asking is NOT a sign of weakness, it is a sign of wisdom and willingness. Speak up and let us know what you want our Help with today. Ask with confidence and boldness knowing that we ADORE you and long to reveal Our love to you in as many ways as possible, without taking away your own joy of accomplishment and creativity. Tell Us the what, and let go of the how. We can take it from there.

We would also encourage you to ask the people in your life for what you want. Asking in this way is not a demand, nor an expectation. It is an invitation to intimate connection. Release people from needing to read your mind. Speak up. Ask, ask, ask - without attachment to what their answer is and without timidness. As you say, "put it out there" and give people a chance to participate in your life. You may be surprised at the number of yes's that come when you begin to practice asking on a regular basis.

51

Without a Strong No, You've Got a Weak Yes

Before you choose to do anything, ask me if your choice is in accord with mine. If you are sure that it is, there will be no fear. Fear is always a sign of strain, arising whenever what you want conflicts with what you do.

-A Course in Miracles

"Spiritual" people seem to have a difficult time saying no - well, until they are resentful and pissed off or sick and exhausted. But We urge you to "let your yeas be yeas and your nays be nays." A simple "no thank you" is an acceptable answer. Seldom is there any need for further explanation or justification.

Some of the reasons that many miracle workers do not say "no" are . . .

* Your ego is flattered that they want you so you say yes
* Martyr/Savior syndrome - trying to save EVERYONE
* Perfectionism - "I'm the only one who can do it right anyhow."
* FEAR that this is your only chance and you'll never be asked again

* Believing they won't like you if you say no - loss of approval or love
* Thinking spiritual people always say yes to every request
* Free-floating guilt

and so many more.

All these little yes's can cost you your ultimate YES in the long-run. For instance, if your goal is inner-peace, harmony, intimate time with your loved ones, resting in God - then saying "yes" to an endless array of invitations and projects that have nothing to do with peace and intimacy can cost you that goal. So many of you LOVE calling yourselves "creators" of your own experience and then you act as if you are not the one who is creating your own schedule. You cannot have it both ways. If you ARE the creator, then learning to calmly say "no thank you" is a miracle working skill worth cultivating.

Most overwhelmed people are doing it to themselves out of fear and endless ambition. This is not the free flow of the Tao. This is not the path to TRUE success. It is a path to suffering needlessly. And the place to start practicing is in saying no to the ego when it starts to get you preoccupied with meaningless things.

52

How Easy Can You LET It Get?

ο ο ο ο ο ο ο ο ο ο ο ο ο ο ο ο ο ο ο ο ο ο ο ο ο ο ο ο ο ο

When you have learned how to decide with God, all decisions become as easy and as right as breathing. There is no effort, and you will be led as gently as if you were being carried down a quiet path in summer.

-A Course in Miracles

We've noticed that you sometimes have a tendency to make things so much harder than they are - mostly through your own inner-thoughts and concepts. So often We see you bracing yourself for some upcoming situation that you've decided is going to be a struggle before it's even really begun. You allow your own past experiences or the stories of other people or even just the world struggle mythology direct your thoughts and vibrations.

We would love to see less of your preparation for what could go wrong and more imagining things going right. The simple fact is that you tend to get what you prepare for and what you expect. Have you noticed that the endless energy that goes into preparation for war is never in vain? You create what you prepare for. And what We want to let you know is that if you as an individual took a certain percentage of your weekly financial income and used it to buy party supplies every week "just in case a party broke out" that would not be in vain either.

We guarantee you that parties would begin to break out quite regularly in your home.

So take a look to see if you are unconsciously bracing yourself for some imagined future struggle or hardship. You may even be telling yourself some stressful story about how difficult it will be for you when your body reaches a certain age. You prepare for the stories you tell yourself and in doing so you set up a momentum which would otherwise not be there.

Make a shift today and begin preparing for all the unknown but now totally expected joy, love, laughter, happy friendships and all manner of ease in living that We want to shower you with. Stop making things so hard and complicated. Let it be easy.

53

Above the Law

Grace is the natural state of every Child of God. When he is not in a state of grace, he is out of his natural environment and does not function well . . . a child of God is happy only when she knows she is with God.

-A Course in Miracles

There is a way to live in this world in which you do not live by the legalistic ways of cause and effect. It is a state where you reap when you have not even sown. This is the state of Grace. There is plenty of room in the state of Grace because the masses prefer the lower vibrational kingdoms of cause and effect where they can keep their personal preferences and the illusion of control.

In order to enter the state of Grace, you must give up control and personal power exchanging them for surrender and Christic power. In Grace, all personal credit goes out the window and one must let go of self-initiated plans and strategizing. There is a dissolving of external goals and a more relaxed and submissive mentality takes center stage. This is the place of "effortless accomplishment" that We speak of - but it is often not the things that you thought needed to be accomplished because you live as vessel of the Light rather than as the chooser.

You can tell when you are in the state of Grace because faith has replaced fear. You have reached a state where you know that nothing, absolutely nothing belongs to you and so you enjoy what is present without identifying yourself with it. You give without even thinking and graciously receive without feeling indebted. Where you will live, how you will live, what your work will be, who will be with you - all of these you trust to Grace and not to your list-making. You are in the God-stream. If there is fear present, you are not in the state of Grace and are still living under the laws of cause and effect. You cannot earn your way into Grace because it is a gift of God. But in order to receive it you must let go of your way, you must let go of being right, you must let go of judging according to appearances. Until you do this, you have made Grace unwelcome in your heart and must continue to live by the laws of sowing and reaping.

54

Pay Attention to the Man Behind the Curtain

o o o o o o o o o o o o o o o o o o o o o o o o o o o o o o o o o

Prepare you now for the undoing of what never was . . . put yourself not in charge of this, for you cannot distinguish between advance and retreat. Some of your greatest advances you have judged as failures, and some of your deepest retreats you have evaluated as success.

-A Course in Miracles

Please miracle worker, do not confuse excitement with happiness, nor boredom with peace. This is one of the tricks of the ego mind that is most insidious because it is so subtle. You must learn to look with inner-vision rather than physical sight if you are to see Truth. Many times your excitement causes you to allow ego goals to mix in with spiritual principles because the ego gets very excited when it thinks it will "get" what it wants. But this is NOT happiness.

To take one of the extreme examples, Hitler was a man who was quite adept at using the law of attraction to create his "vision" and he was a person who was not afraid to DREAM BIG! He was extremely goal-oriented, excited and had a great deal of passion for his vision. AND he was the hero of his story - he thought he was in the right! In his own way he thought that he had a kind of "god" on his side. In this way he was using many of the contemporary self-help spiritualized gimmicks that are so popular in a world run by egoic greed, fear and attack thoughts. Obviously he had moved as far from sanity and spiritual principle as one can go.

Many of you get off track by making too much of Universal and/ or spiritual laws and too little of Universal Spiritual Principles. Too much focus on laws leads to legalistic thinking and lack of compassion for self and others. You can be miserable and yet quite excited at the same time and not even realize it. Sometimes the very religious can fall prey to over-emphasis on so-called religious laws and become quite judgmental and self-righteous. Even Brother Jesus was condemned by the "legalists" for breaking religious laws because he let spiritual LOVE be His driving force - and there is no greater principle than love. The Course makes all of this very simple and it too is quite goal-oriented. The goal is God, the goal is inner-peace, the goal is forgiveness, the goal is the healing of the mind that tends to believe in separation.

I do not think big, I think divinely for God is my only goal today.

55

Mind Your Mind

o o o o o o o o o o o o o o o o o o o o o o o o o o o o o o o

To heal is to make happy. I have told you to think of how many opportunities you have had to gladden yourself, and how many you have refused. This is the same thing as telling you that you have refused to heal yourself.

-A Course in Miracles

Miracle worker, never underestimate the viciousness of the ego and its desire to have you focus your attention on the things that are the most disturbing to you. It is not merely what you focus on, but what is even more important is WHO you have chosen as your guide to seeing.

When the ego is your companion, everything will seem bleak and dark. When the Holy Spirit is your Guide, then even when things seem darkest, the Light in you will shine outward and you will be able to find your way home. Remember when you are going through hell to KEEP GOING - do not sit down and languish in the misery of it all.

Do not be lazy about this. Be vigilant in CHOOSING happiness and in CHOOSING Who will be your Guide each day. You do not have to control your thoughts, but with the help of the Holy Spirit you can learn how to effectively GUIDE them so that you will take advantage of all the opportunities for healing that are available to you each day. Remember that God's will for you is happiness, not suffering.

56

Paying and Getting

○ ○

If paying is equated with getting, you will set the price low but demand a high return. You will have forgotten, however, that to price is to value, so that your return is in proportion to your judgment of worth. If paying is associated with giving it cannot be perceived as loss, and the reciprocal relationship of giving and receiving will be recognized. The price will then be set high, because of the value of the return.

-A Course in Miracles

So much of your world is based on bargaining with your brother. This has a tendency to inadvertantly make you hard-hearted in various aspects of all of your relationships - the unfortunate outcome of this is a loss of peace and an even greater loss of your sense of Self. Your happiest relationships are almost always those in which your main focus is to give - this is why your relationships with your animals and babies induce so much joy within you.

Even the vibrational frequency of the words "pay" and "get" are very dense and fear-inducing because they operate on the scarcity principle. We would like you to replace them with the words "give" and "receive" or even "contribute" and "accept" because these words work from the higher frequencies of the abundance principle.

In your world you will usually think of this in terms of money alone, but We are encouraging you to expand FAR beyond that to every relationship in your life. Even in your romantic relationships there is a tendency to think somewhat in terms of bartering and bargaining for perceived needs and wants. Let it go. It causes nothing but pain and resentments.

Two questions to ask yourself frequently that will help you along this path are:

1. What can I contribute here without expectation or attachment to outcomes?
2. In this moment, can I let go of the concept of getting and simply be open to receive?

57

Walk Only Through The Open Doors

o o o o o o o o o o o o o o o o o o o o o o o o o o o o o o

I seek but what belongs to me in truth.

-A Course in Miracles

So much time and energy is wasted banging on closed doors until your hands are bloody stumps. So many humans want what does not want them and this is the cause of tremendous suffering. We see so many of you hurling yourselves like battering rams against locked concrete doors that We felt the need to give this ridiculously obvious lesson today.

There is a beautiful life waiting for you behind every open door - it is the life that is uniquely yours. Remember that this is a highly individualized curriculum and not a "one-size-fits-all" lifestyle.

The world and culture hypnotizes you into wanting what IT wants you to want. You destiny is to awaken from this mesmerism in order to find your LIFE. You are too grand for a lifestyle. Lifestyles are the ego's replacement for an authentic LIFE. Accept no shabby substitutes for the life that God wants you to have.

It is extremely difficult to get and keep a lifestyle that is not really your soul's authentic match. Choose instead to walk through the open doors that lead to LIFE and you will find that it is truly effortless. Yes, there will be work, but it will not feel like the struggling "sweat of the brow" type and you may not even think that it is work at all. From now on, begin to notice the doors that are opening to you and if it calls your spirit to it, walk through.

58

Calm the Fuck Down

o o o o o o o o o o o o o o o o o o o o o o o o o o o o o o o o o

Simply do this: Be still, and lay aside all thoughts of what you are and what God is; all concepts you have learned about the world; all images you hold about yourself. Empty your mind of everything it thinks is either true or false, or good or bad, of every thought it judges worthy, and all the ideas of which it is ashamed. Hold onto nothing. Do not bring with you one thought the past has taught, nor one belief you ever learned before from anything. Forget this world, forget this course, and come with wholly empty hands unto your God.

-A Course in Miracles

Just let it all go, for even an instant. Let the thoughts slow down and merely observe them moving through like clouds on a windy day. In this moment there is no need to choose a thought, nor to think positively or creatively - no need to hold a thought. Nor is it necessary to get rid of any thoughts. All that you need do is know that you are not these thoughts. For a few moments cease to identify with them. Just notice them without attachment - nothing to do, or get, or fix, or change - nothing to figure out.

Exhale. Let your shoulders drop as you relax on the exhale. Open up. Be willing to receive. Breathe deeply and let your gut fill up with oxygen and prana as it gently expands. Focus your attention there.

This is the place of connection. This is the place of nourishment, of connection to the Mother Source, of birthing new ideas and it does not come from personal effort. Your part is to midwife whatever is wanting to come through. Your part is to not interfere with this perfectly normal process.

The mind will confuse you. The heart will lie to you. They are both horrible masters, but miraculous servants of Spiritual Wisdom. The gut will always lead you to that Wisdom - but, you must be willing to get quiet enough to spend some time there. This is one of those times.

59

Pity Party of One!

o o o o o o o o o o o o o o o o o o o o o o o o o o o o o o o

You who are sometimes sad and sometimes angry; who sometimes feel your just due is not given you, and your best efforts meet with lack of appreciation and even contempt; give up these foolish thoughts! They are too small and meaningless to occupy your holy mind an instant longer.

-A Course in Miracles

Self-pity is another cover for the rage that lies beneath it. It is the ego's attempt to hold onto yet another mask. Self-pity is by definition a state of separation and aloneness for no one can join you there - ever. Pouting and perceptual temper tantrums only hurt the mind that engages in them.

So little miracle worker, We have no problem with throwing yourself a pity party once or twice a year for a few hours while you wallow on the sofa watching bad movies and eating ice cream out of the container. But never let it last more than an evening. To indulge this kind of victim consciousness thinking for any longer than that is to activate the magnetic laws of the Universe and soon you'll find that ridiculous experience that some parents threaten of "I'll give you something to cry about!" Only in this case, YOU give yourself something to cry about through your unconscious use of the law.

What We have found time after time is that those beings who have the most reasons for self-pity rarely engage in it - while those who have the most to be grateful for are often the most sloppy in allowing their attention to move them into a story of being "unfairly treated" every time someone, something, or they themselves do not fulfill the "role" that they have assigned to them. Remember to guard your mind miracle worker. Do not shut Us out and leave the ego in through your lack of diligence during trying times. Remove your allegiance to the ego and clean up your consciousness again by moving into outrageous praise and appreciation for whatever good is in your life today. Pollyanna called this "the glad game" and it is one of the most powerful practices you have at your disposal. The only question is, are you willing to be happy or are you not finished suffering yet?

60

Nothing To Do But Receive

o o o o o o o o o o o o o o o o o o o o o o o o o o o o o o o o o o o

When the body is kept bustling about without stop, it becomes fatigued. When the mind is overworked without stop, it becomes worried, and worry causes exhaustion. The nature of water is that it becomes clear when left alone and becomes still when undisturbed. When it becomes bottled up and cannot flow, it also cannot remain clear. It is the symbol of heavenly virtue.

-Chaung Tzu

Make time today for stillness. Become very quiet and still knowing that there is nothing to get, nothing to fix, nothing to change. There is nothing for you to do but receive. You cannot "get" today, you can only open to receive.

For a period of time leave behind your strategies and plans. Let go of trying to figure out WHAT TO DO to get what you want. Stop the mental fighting and resistance even for five minutes and let yourself drift away from your present concerns. This is the practice of radical non-interference.

As you sit in quiet stillness, your mind will begin to settle. When you cease whipping the mind into a frenzy, the sediment settles to the bottom and there is crystal clarity and peace. Give Us all your plans and goals to handle today. Your job is to simply show up with a calm mind and an open heart.

61

This Is Not A Test

o o o o o o o o o o o o o o o o o o o o o o o o o o o o o o

You do experience guilt, but you have no idea why. On the contrary, you associate it with a weird assortment of "ego ideals" which the ego claims you have failed.

-A Course in Miracles

This is a journey. You cannot fail because it is not a test. You CAN get lost for a while, but then you merely need to find your north star again and return to the highlighted route. It doesn't matter how you got lost, how lost you are or whose "fault" it was. Just get back on the road.

62

The Love Walk

o o o o o o o o o o o o o o o o o o o o o o o o o o o o o o o o

Love is the way I walk in gratitude . . . let our brothers (and sisters) lean their tired heads against our shoulders as they rest a while. We offer thanks for them. For if we can direct them to the peace that we would find, the way is opening to us at last.

-A Course in Miracles

Only what you would share with another is worth having at all. There is nothing worthwhile that you can ever keep for yourself and hope to find the happiness and peace that you seek. Each day is another chance to walk in shadows or walk in Light; to walk in fear or walk in Love. It is not possible to walk in love while holding yourself apart from those around you.

Teaching and sharing are the greatest gifts of every miracle worker and are the means to a lasting happiness that the things of this world can never give. The world has disappointed you over and over again with its tiny and temporary "treasures" and this you have surely seen by now.

Miracle worker, this is the time for your love walk to take precedent over all the idols that you have sought in the past. Today you will understand that what you teach, what you share, what you give, is what you yourself will receive. This kind of giving does not deplete but generates. God loves the world through you. God needs your hands, your feet and your voice to do His will and God's will is perfect happiness for all. It is NOT a path of sacrifice - it is the party to end all parties! Dancing and singing are definitely encouraged today.

63

Ebb and Flow

o o o o o o o o o o o o o o o o o o o o o o o o o o o o o o o o

. . . trust would settle every problem now.

-A Course in Miracles

Some of you spiritual types really do crack Us up! You stress yourselves out over perfectly natural happenings and then spin yourselves into a frenzy fighting against a temporary and yet perfectly normal energy movement. You try so hard to "create and manifest" an ocean in which the tide only comes in and never goes out, even though this would actually drown you and all your family and friends.

Energy systems rise and fall. This is how it is meant to be. Night follows day and winter follows the summer. "For everything there is a season" and yet you fight, fight, fight against the seasons and make yourselves crazy thinking that WINTER IS WRONG AND BAD AND UNBEARABLE AND SHOULD NOT HAPPEN!! You've even managed to build a system that resists the notion of rest altogether by creating a 24/7 world. There was a time when stores would close on Sundays, television went off the air during the late-night hours, there was no internet to keep your shopping ability ever-active, certain foods were not available during the winter months. This created more balance and harmony in your lives and there was far less need for "sleep aids" or mood stabilizers. Many of you are entertaining yourselves to death. But you are free to stop at any time you decide.

Do not panic when the tide goes out in some area of your life. Stop thinking that it is something horribly wrong which must be fixed or healed. This is the perfect time to rest, to allow, to renew your spirit and deepen your connection to God and your inner-Life. Spring WILL come again - it is built into the system. The tide WILL come in again - it's built into the system. In energy systems, the more you resist the current one, the longer it seems to last. When you relax your resistance, time itself begins to be a non-issue and peace is restored in your now.

64

I'm the One!!

If you inspire joy and others react to you with joy, even though you are not experiencing joy yourself there must be something in you that is capable of producing it. If it is in you and can produce joy, and if you see that it does produce joy in others, you must be dissociating it in yourself.

-A Course in Miracles

It is up to you to make yourself happy. No one has been or will be assigned to you in that way. No one is coming to save you. No one is coming to make you happy. Many many people are on the way into your life, but none of them can or will save you from your own thoughts, perceptions and choices. You are the one.

If you can really see the blessing that this is, your life will take on a peace and joy that truly does pass all understanding because if YOU are the one, then you always know where to find the one who makes you happy. Every child of God is given the capacity to create joy and you can see that at times you have stimulated the joy in others, but you did not PLACE it there. It was still their choice, their decision.

So when you are not feeling fully joyful yourself it is good remember that you still have the talent for joy that God gave you and you must ask yourself why you are not using it on yourself. What excuse are you using to keep you from experiencing the comfort of your own abilities? Are you putting the responsibility on someone or something outside of you? This is a very popular suffering game and it is definitely beneath you miracle worker. You deserve so much better and no one can give it to you except your Self.

65

Just Do One Thing

o o o o o o o o o o o o o o o o o o o o o o o o o o o o o o o

It is, perhaps, not easy to perceive that self-initiated plans are but defenses with the purpose all of them were made to realize. They are the means by which a frightened mind would undertake its own protection, at the cost of truth.

-A Course in Miracles

Living "one day at a time" is the only true choice. Can you live more than one day at a time? Of course not, but your mind can TRY to live an entire imaginary future right now. Sometimes you overwhelm yourselves before you've even left your chair - and while you are "multi-tasking" you are not really present with anything except the chaos of your planning mind.

Today, practice slowing down the mind as you "just do one thing" at a time. This is your peace today. As your mind tries to paralyze you with the "big picture" and overwhelm you with plans and strategies in which you try to control your world, focus instead on the thing right in front of you to do. Just do that one thing. And when that one is done, go on to the next one and just do that one thing. Even when washing the dishes, wash one dish at a time and be present with THAT dish rather than mentally whirling into the next 10 things to be done.

This is a truly meditative practice. You are learning to gently guide your own mind, to calm your fears and regulate your own nervous system. The benefits of this very simple practice will have amazingly beneficial results the more that you practice it and you will find that even your progress in achieving external goals makes tremendous gains when you learn to slow down and focus this way.

66

Where Is Your Faith?

o o o o o o o o o o o o o o o o o o o o o o o o o o o o o o

Why is it strange to you that faith can move mountains? This is indeed a little feat for such a power. For faith can keep the Son of God in chains as long as he believes he is in chains. And when he is released from them it will be simply because he no longer believes in them.

-A Course in Miracles

Everyone has faith and has faith all the time. What tends to shift and change is WHAT each one has faith in. When you have faith in the things of this world, you ask for suffering because all the things of the world are temporary and ever-changing. Place your faith in what is eternal and changeless and you will find the joy that you deserve.

Principles are eternal and changeless. They are your north star. Teachings change, evolve and grow. They are like maps of the terrain - they change because the terrain changes over time. Teachings and techniques can be very helpful, but they can also be complicated, difficult to remember and may not be equally applicable to all situations. Spiritual principles apply everywhere equally and are extremely simple. Here is today's spiritual principle made into an easy practice:

Extend Love
Demonstrate Peace

As you do this, you are putting your faith in simple eternal principles rather than in the ever-changing world of people, places and things. In any situation that arises today in which you are uncertain, remind yourself, "My only goal here is to extend love and demonstrate peace." This is POWERFUL act of faith.

67

Courage and Confidence Now

○ ○

The thing you're waiting to have happen before you make the commitment, happens after you make the commitment.

-Reverend Terry

You may think that if you had more confidence or were more fearless that you would do more in life and achieve more, as in . . .

* If I had more courage I would ask for a promotion and a raise.
* If I had more self-esteem I would invite him to dinner.
* If I had more discipline I'd go to the gym.
* If I had more faith I'd start the business I've been dreaming of starting.
* If I were not so afraid I would tell my mate how I feel.

But this is just another of the delay tactics of the ego. The reality is that courage and confidence are gained by the doing. The action comes first and the courage and confidence are the fruits of that labor, not the other way around. If these character aspects are not natural to your personality, they must be cultivated one action at a time.

We will guide you to the right actions if you will go inside and ask for direction.

You are completely safe as long as you are completely unconcerned about your own readiness, but maintain a consistent trust in mine.

-A Course in Miracles

68

The Graduate Level Love Walk

o o o o o o o o o o o o o o o o o o o o o o o o o o o o o o o o

You can place any relationship under His care and be sure that it will not result in pain, if you offer Him your willingness to have it serve no need but His. All the guilt in it arises from your use of it. All the love from His.

-A Course in Miracles

Have you suffered enough? We will be asking that from time to time since so many of you have a tremendous tolerance and endless energy for mental suffering. Of course the word "suffering" may seem extreme to you, but We would like to point out that even mild dissatisfaction is a kind of unnecessary suffering that you are quite tolerant of at times.

But, there is no area in which mental suffering is greater than when it comes to your "special" relationships. This is because you whole world actually encourages you to go into them full of ego projections of guilt, conditions and a mentality that has to do with getting rather than giving. When it comes to relationships, many of you have the mantra of "I want, I want, I want, I need, I need, I need" and in an atmosphere based on attraction you magnetize relationships that are full of the vibration of unmet wants and needs. They are the exact mirror of the consciousness that demonstrated them.

When it comes to relationships, the simplest and humblest prayers are the best. When you get to graduate level spiritual maturity, things do not become more complicated, they actually get simpler and simpler the farther you go.

Holy Spirit, if you have someone you want to love through me. Here I am. I am willing. I will not try to get someone or to create something that will serve my needs but instead am making myself available to whomever YOU want to love through me. In fact, I am not going to try to get anything but I am open to receive whatever you want to give. I want to be a blessing - please make it fun, make it simple, make it easy for me to see Your hand in it. Teach me how to love with total joy and abandon. I am ready to give and receive all that is part of the Divine Plan for my life now.

69

The Excellence of Mediocrity

o o o o o o o o o o o o o o o o o o o o o o o o o o o o o o o o o

Make friends with mediocrity.

-Byron Katie

Yes, it's one of those times when we need to poke you with a stick again, just to torment you into a new way of thinking and being. So take a deep breath and walk with Us.

Mediocrity and excellence are only concepts - they have nothing to do with reality as God created it. And the fact is, they are extremely stressful concepts that cause tremendous suffering in your society. People who are "going for excellence" tend to be filled with stress and are often downright mean to those around them, feeling quite justified in their cruelty because they are surrounded by "lesser" types who just don't understand how important it is to be perfect. And they are equally cruel to themselves in their own thinking. Yet, they rarely go for excellence in love which is really the only excellent thing that exists. Anyone who understands reality ONLY goes for excellence when it comes to love, which means treating those around you with kindness, patience and mercy.

We say that in the other areas of your life, embrace mediocrity, embrace average, embrace normal. This is the end of the ego's insane search for specialness but it is the beginning of your freedom and peace.

Excellence is the belief that there is a competition going on and this is simply not true. Look at the ordinary world around you. The sunrise and sunset is perfectly mediocre, average and ordinary and it is not TRYING to do anything. Yet each one is spectacular in its own way and there is no need for comparison to any other one. Notice how your pets do not strive for excellence and yet you adore them and provide for every one of their needs. This is how God thinks of you as well.

We are pushing this word mediocrity in order to push your buttons a bit so you can get out of the prisons you build for yourselves. We don't "spiritualize" things into a "positive" wording in order to make you more comfortable because then ego just cons you into staying in the same old cell but with a prettier wall color. This "mediocrity" we are teaching is not about "not caring" but it is about not competing. In face, We say show up, show up on time, be prepared, keep your word and agreements, do what you know to do, practice kindness, make the best of what is available and let go of the rest.

Pride will not produce miracles.

-A Course in Miracles

70

Let the Love In

○ ○

Perhaps you think that different kinds of love are possible. Perhaps you think there is a kind of love for this, a kind of love for that; a way of loving one, another way of loving still another. Love is one. It has no separate divergencies and no distinctions . . . if you achieve the faintest glimmering of what love means today, you have advanced in distance without measure and in time beyond the count of years to your release.

-A Course in Miracles

We have already told you that a "get" mentality is not a receptive mentality - and receptivity is something that you would do well to work on within your own consciousness. Many of you profess how available to love you are and that the problem is how love is not available to you . . . until someone who IS available is standing in front of you. THEN, you find out just who it is that is really not available. You pray and pray for something or someone and then so quickly reject the answer when it comes.

You have all kinds of reasons and excuses for keeping love out and it all has to do with your "pictures" of how it should look. But true love will rarely fit into the neat little box you've made for it. Love is messy and sometimes quite uncomfortable. Love requires a willingness to mature and grow. Love will not respect your comfort zone. Love breaks the heart, but it breaks it open.

Love is already in you, there is no need to try to get it - but, if you are saving your love for the "right" time, the "right" person or situation, then you would do well to remember that what you withhold is always withheld from you. It is the mirror principle of life at work.

We're not talking about form here - letting in the love does not necessarily mean dating someone, going into business with them, marrying them or any other external action that the ego tries to tell you it means. It's actually something much scarier than any of those things . . . it's letting love into your heart without defining or labeling it with a name. Be honest with yourself today. Are you truly open to receive love whatever form or formlessness it comes in today?

71

Trust

○ ○

When this power has once been experienced, it is impossible to trust one's own petty strength again. Who would attempt to fly with the tiny wings of a sparrow when the mighty power of an eagle has been given him? And who would place her strength in the shabby offerings of the ego when the gifts of God are laid before her?

-A Course in Miracles

Please do not attempt to run your own life today. Simply choose to be happy and to do all you can to increase your own awareness of joy. We need HAPPY miracle workers in order to do God's will. We will take care of the details of your life if you will go about being happy and sharing that joy with others today.

Whatever needs to be done, give it to Us and We will not only accompany you, but We will also go ahead of you, behind you, to your right and to your left, above and below, making straight the way as you walk in love and faith. Refuse to worry today. Refuse to take anxious thought.

This is a day to practice trusting in the Power of the Divine Architect to run your life, remembering that ONLY God's plan will work.

72

Constructive Criticism is a Myth

o o o o o o o o o o o o o o o o o o o o o o o o o o o o o o o o o o

The alertness of the ego to the errors of other egos is not the kind of vigilance the Holy Spirit would have you maintain.

-A Course in Miracles

Love does not tear down, it builds up. This includes not only the tearing down of others but the tearing down of yourself as well. Humility is encouraged - condemnation and shame and guilt are completely unwelcome. All criticism has judgment in it and therefore there is no way that it is capable of being truly constructive - it is always destructive to some degree.

Guidance and gentle correction are quite different from criticism, mostly because of the intent of the heart. Search your heart frequently to question your motives. Before you offer any guidance or correction to another, stop to sense the energy of the other person and of the situation to see if there is an opening to receive it. Ask Holy Spirit to enter the relationship and then speak only if guided to do so and then proceed in the most gentle way possible. Everyone is in process and though harsh interventions are SOMEtimes called for, it is extremely rare that they are truly helpful.

And it is very helpful to remember that positive feedback is always more beneficial than corrective advice. However, if you give enormous amounts of uplifting positive feedback to another child of God, when you DO have some correction to give, the opening to receive it is much greater than if you are one who only has something to say when you DO NOT like something. Be one who uplifts, one who supports, one who soothes, one who acknowledges, one who sees the good and praises it. Then, on those infrequent times when you are required to give some guidance, there is a greater chance that there will be an opening to receive you.

73

Manage Your Focus

○ ○

*I am responsible for what I see. I choose the feelings I experience,
and I decide upon the goal I would achieve . . . deceive yourself
no longer that you are helpless in the face of what is done to you.
Acknowledge but that you have been mistaken, and all effects of
your mistakes will disappear.*

-A Course in Miracles

Where is your attention and what consciousness are you activating
within you now? The choice is yours though you may tell the story
of how other people and situations are the cause and that you have
no choice. Do not give in to this kind of temptation. Remember that
YOU can always choose what you will focus on, and what you focus on
will become your dominant consciousness.

Many many things may happen in a day, but what you give your
attention to is your responsibility. Keep it simple - there is love and
there is fear. Lump everything into one category or another - love feels
good, fear does not. That's really all you need to know. You are either
activating a love consciousness or a fear consciousness, based on what
you give your attention to and how.

If you are in a situation which requires you to focus on something
which activates fear within you, ask Holy Spirit to be your Guide to

seeing and miracles are bound to happen. Managing what you give your attention to and how is a powerful way of taking responsibility for your conscious focus! In times of great trial We suggest that 3 times a day you set aside time to make a list of gratitude and appreciation. No matter how seemingly small and insignificant the things on the list may be, they have great power to neutralize the consciousness of fear. Be vigilant miracle worker! YOU are worth the effort.

74

It's a God Thing

Miracles are a kind of exchange. Like all expressions of love, which are always miraculous in the true sense, the exchange reverses the physical laws. They bring more love both to the giver and the receiver.

-A Course in Miracles

It's time now to move to a new level of experience. In this phase you will begin to fulfill your miraculous function on a much more regular basis because you will learn how little you know and more importantly how little you need to know. In fact, We usually like to keep you on a strictly "need to know" basis so that you are less apt to interfere with the Divine Plan.

It is not important for you to understand what is happening all the time . . . this is the purpose of faith. Many of your assignments (yes, you will come to see that there are "assignments" that you came to fulfill - class assignments which have to do with the exchange of miracles) will make no sense to you at all and in fulfilling them your life may look very strange to others . . . or it may not. But if you resist the temptation to judge according to appearances and instead trust what you call intuition, your life will begin to FEEL very right regardless of how it appears to you or anyone else.

This is the time in which your experience of Love will seep into every aspect of your life and when that happens, weird may become your new normal. We enjoy the way that one of you explains the unexplainable to those around her by simply saying, "It's a God thing" and leaving it at that. This may be a very helpful affirmation for you to try on now as well.

75

Sowing the Seeds of Love

o o o o o o o o o o o o o o o o o o o o o o o o o o o o o o

The miracle worker must have genuine respect for true cause and effect as a necessary condition for the miracle to occur.

-A Course in Miracles

Affection is a feeling. LOVE only comes ALIVE through action. Humans tend to get caught up in the mistake of needing to FEEL affection before you are willing to ACT out your love. Once again, this is the reversal of the seed and harvest effect. You are waiting for a harvest before you are willing to plant a seed. Hopeless!

Take the loving action FIRST and the feeling of affection will follow. Don't wait to feel like it because most of the time you won't feel like it.

This is true in your actions with others and in your actions with yourself. You may not FEEL love toward yourself, but if you ACT in a loving way towards yourself, your heart will begin to follow the actions. Cause THEN effect - that's the order. Make this a day in which you practice taking loving actions - this is a way of sowing seeds and that is a good way to think of it. Make it a game. See how many people you an uplift, acknowledge, appreciate, soothe, make smile and generally contribute joy to today - do NOT exclude yourself from this process!

76

Refuse to be Offended

o o o o o o o o o o o o o o o o o o o o o o o o o o o o o o o

Each day, each hour, every instant, I am choosing what I want to look upon, the sounds I want to hear, the witnesses to what I want to be the truth for me. Today I choose to look upon what Christ would have me see, to listen to God's Voice, and seek the witnesses to what is true in God's creation.

-A Course in Miracles

Some of you are very touchy, and this is a great cause of mental anguish. Being offended is actually a choice you make - it is an interpretation of what someone said or did, didn't say or didn't do. And no matter how "obvious" the offense is, you are always always at choice in what you will make of it - what you will do with it.

This is why it is so important each morning to set the intention of how you want to FEEL all day long. This is a powerful choice to make and once you make it, mind will begin to focus on and gather up the evidence that will support that choice. You will overlook the things that interfere with your goal and focus on the things that align with it. If you do not consciously set this goal, then your mind will automatically choose whatever is your default set point. If your default is to focus on upsetting things, then mind will automatically do that. If you default is to focus on whatever is good and right and uplifting, then mind will make that the goal. Once you CHOOSE to not be offended in life, your experience of peace and joy will begin to expand rapidly.

Decide that from now on you will assume the best about people and situations - that you will be one whose dominant consciousness is one of MERCY toward anyone who does not seem to be acting from their highest self. Give people the benefit of the doubt. Do not focus on their guilt but instead, pray that their pain be comforted as you release them to Divine Care.

Great peace have they which love thy law: and nothing shall offend them.

-Psalm 119:165

77

Drink in The Vision

○ ○

Happy dreams come true, not because they are dreams, but only because they are happy. And so they must be loving. Their message is, "Thy Will be done," and not, "I want it otherwise."

-A Course in Miracles

You must always try to remember that the Universal Will is for your total happiness and joy, though it may not be about getting what you thought you wanted or needed. The Divine Will is always better and more satisfying than what the flesh wants. When your goals and visions create stress, struggle and strain, you must be engaged in self-will again and are trying to make things happen rather than allowing things to happen from a Higher Order.

When this occurs, it is best to step back again and refocus on the JOY of the deeper vision. Happy dreams are infused with the Universal Joy which is the glue that holds all things together. Find the feeling of joy again as you stop trying to micro-manage meaningless minutiae. Just for now, let go of the DOing part and drink in the vision. Completely let go of the HOW and simply enjoy the WHAT for a while again. Also, try not to get so attached to the specific forms but rather stimulate the FEELINGS you want to cultivate through this vision.

True visionaries rarely know the "how", but the "what" is so deeply compelling within them that all the necessary resources, people, opportunities and ideas begin to gravitate towards them, or the visionary herself is drawn along to the next open door. It's a God thing.

78

What Does it Mean???

o o o o o o o o o o o o o o o o o o o o o o o o o o o o o o o

I do not know what anything, including this, means. And so I do not know how to respond to it. And I will not use my own past learning as the light to guide me now.

-A Course in Miracles

Can you imagine how much time and energy would be saved if you gave up all attempts to try to interpret the meaning of the happenings in your life as well as the behaviors of other people? How many endless and fruitless conversations have you had with others with each of you trying to figure out what someone meant when they did or didn't say this or that? How much time and energy spent trying to figure out why this or that happened in your life? And the ego always wants you to use what it "learned" in the past to apply to your now. But the ego has only learned about defensiveness and hardness of heart so it's lessons guarantee yet another unhappy outcome.

This is such a tremendous waste when you realize that you have a perfect Guide to miracles in your present. This requires radical faith and trust. It is the decision NOT to judge the present. It is the decision to ASK Holy Spirit to guide you into PEACE NOW.

If you decide that you do not know what anything means, how can you be upset? When you don't know what anything means, then you are open to seeing beyond appearances and you have become teachable.

I don't know what anything means, but I am willing and ready to be taught.

Holy Spirit, guide my thoughts and show me what You would have me see.

I place all things in Your hands today and I want only God's will for all.

79

I Shouldn't Have To!!

o o o o o o o o o o o o o o o o o o o o o o o o o o o o o o o o o

You give but to yourself. Who understands what giving means must laugh at the idea of sacrifice.

-A Course in Miracles

An absent positive will become an assumed negative. The complimentary thought that you think but don't give will be an assumed criticism. That's just how the ego mind tends to operate. Think of it this way, if you got a radically different new haircut and not a single person said anything to you about it, you would tend to automatically assume that everyone hated it or that you are so insignificant that no one notices anything about you one way or the other. The ego always fills in the blanks with attack thoughts.

Very little destroys the love in relationships as neatly as the thought, "I shouldn't have to!" Many of you use this as a hideous little mantra which not only destroys the love in your relationships but it also makes you feel like shit because it cultivates deep resentments. When you withhold your acknowledgments and kind words, when you stop sharing your thoughts and feelings with loved ones, all because you think they SHOULD know without you saying it, YOU are the one who will suffer most. Again, what you withhold will be withheld from YOU.

It is a HUGE MYTH that someone can "give too much" in a relationship. It's never happened in all the history of humankind . . . not ever. Many many have made deals of "giving to get" which did not pan out, but no one has EVER given too much love or acknowledgment to another human being. If you feel ripped-off at the end of a relationship because you "gave too much" of yourself, look back honestly at how you were giving with huge expectations of how THEY were supposed to make you feel or give to you, but didn't. This is not true giving - this is paying in order to get.

And remember, real love often says "no" - love does not always go along with, love certainly does not always approve of behaviors, nor does love mean that physical closeness remains. Love acknowledges and uplifts the ESSENCE of who someone is, not necessarily what they are doing. You can support a person without supporting or agreeing with their position. And you do not praise what they are not good at, but you do seek to find the authentic good within them and to bring it center stage. And if you want to invoke the highest and best within someone, the most efficient way to do it is to sincerely thank them, to bless them with words of praise and appreciation and to back it up with actions.

80

You MUST Forgive Yourself

o o o o o o o o o o o o o o o o o o o o o o o o o o o o o o o o o

Forgiveness is the key to happiness. Here is the answer to your search for peace. Here is the key to meaning in a world that seems to make no sense.

-A Course in Miracles

Let it all go miracle worker. To forgive yourself is simply to let go of your story of guilt and punishment. In Heaven there is no forgiveness because there is no judgment, but on earth you have judged yourself quite viciously for your errors. Of course you have made mistakes because all students do. It is part of the learning process to fall down. The problem is that you have felt so ashamed of the mistakes you've made.

Bring them all to the altar within today and as you lay them down be released from them at last. Until you are willing to let this forgiveness wash over you, you are not free to access your full miracle capabilities - there is always a part of you that is hidden and unavailable for God to use.

Ask for and receive the Grace that comes to a humble heart today. There is much that can be accomplished through you now as you are freed from the chains of unforgiveness and guilt. The angels celebrate your release as you now step into the Light to answer the Call.

81

Practice Mercy

○ ○

Help him to lift the heavy burden of sin you laid upon him and he accepted as his own, and toss it lightly and with happy laughter away from him. Press not like thorns against his brow, nor nail him to it, unredeemed and hopeless.

-A Course in Miracles

It must be clear to you by now that when you focus on the errors of those around you, YOU suffer. When you are focusing on the errors of your loved ones, a good image to retain in your mind is that of pressing the crown of thorns into their brow. All of your judgments about them are a refusal to extend them mercy. As you continue to gather up the evidence of the inadequacies of those around you it is the ego methodically planning their mental crucifixion. This goes entirely against your own Divine Nature and because of it you will always feel lonely and separate again.

You would think this would be a habit practiced mostly on strangers, who you see as quite different from yourself, but in reality it is most often practiced with those who are closest to you: co-workers, friends, family members. It is frequently a cherished ego habit of doing this with the romantic "beloved." The ego is intent on disqualifying everyone from being worthy of love, leaving you alone until there is no one left to attack but yourself.

But there is great good news miracle worker! This is nothing more than a mental habit and it can be changed through the Grace of God and the Help of the Holy Spirit, along with your willingness to practice MERCY. Remember that you really DO NOT WANT to press the crown of thorns into the brow of anyone - your real desire is to free them from crucifixion and to wipe away their tears. This is who you are. This is why you came. Remember?

Make it a practice today to take note of how those around you are getting it right, are sufficient, are worthy and are, like you, doing the best they can. Lift them up with your words today. Show them some tenderness, patience and kindness and best of all, if you can, make them laugh.

82

You Matter

o o o o o o o o o o o o o o o o o o o o o o o o o o o o o o o o o

Here is the thought of true humility, which holds no function but that which has been given you. It offers your acceptance of a part assigned to you, without insisting on another role. It does not judge your proper role. It but acknowledges the Will of God is done on earth as well as Heaven.

-A Course in Miracles

We knew what We were getting when We chose you for this assignment. We are not mistaken and things will go so smoothly if you can stop second-guessing Us in Our choice. God's Will IS done in you when you are busy extending love and teaching peace. You teach by demonstrating, not by words. If you are walking in love and walking in peace, you are fulfilling the assignment God gave you.

Please stop the doubting. It's tedious and annoying. Get on with your love walk. When you walk in Love, We are making great use of you. You may wonder how sitting in a cubicle typing meaningless reports or picking up after the children or bringing someone coffee or smiling at a stranger can serve God's plan - but if you are thinking peaceful loving thoughts while you do it, if your intention is to be truly Helpful, then you are working miracles and reversing the downward trend towards fear. NO task is small. All effects of love are maximal.

Let us not fight our function. We did not establish it. It is not our idea. The means are given us by which it will be perfectly accomplished. All that we are asked to do is to accept our part in genuine humility, and not deny with self-deceiving arrogance that we are not worthy. What is given us to do, we have the strength to do. Our minds are suited perfectly to take the part assigned to us by One Who knows us well.

-A Course in Miracles

83

Divine Timing

o o o o o o o o o o o o o o o o o o o o o o o o o o o o o o o

. . . but let me remind you that time and space are under my control.

-A Course in Miracles

Judging. You're always judging.

It is only judgment and lack of faith in the Divine Plan that makes you so impatient. You judge the timing of your life and it causes you great anxiety and tension. Why continue with a habit that is so debilitating, miracle worker? You could be enjoying the ride instead of criticizing the route that's been taken.

There is a story in Genesis chapters 16 & 17 about Sarah and Abraham which is told to remind all generations that what the ego judges as impossible is easy for God. Just because Sarah has always been barren and is 90 years old does not mean that she is too late to give birth to a child. Read the story about Sarah's "plan B" with Abraham's servant Hagar and what a nightmare it turns out to be. When the ego gets impatient it begins strategizing rather than divinely contemplating - and this creates a new and more complicated problem.

We are in no way telling you to "hold on to your dream" or any such nonsense. We ARE advising you to LET GO of your story of what you think is possible. You have no idea - and though you may not have realized this yet, not knowing is peace.

84

Lots Can Happen

o o o o o o o o o o o o o o o o o o o o o o o o o o o o o o o

*Yet the essential thing is learning that you do not know . . .
everything you have taught yourself has made your power more
and more obscure to you.*

-A Course in Miracles

When you come to the place where you are willing to let go of your
perceptions of what you believe is and isn't possible, and can release the
thought that you know what should be happening or what would be
the best thing . . . and you can do it without sadness or embarrassment .
. . in that moment your humility has made a world of miracles possible
for you.

Your part is to show up prepared. To be prepared is to do your
part and let the rest happen as it happens. The best preparation is to
open your heart and mind and simply be present. From there you
may remember that lots can happen beyond what seems reasonable.
Miracles are totally unreasonable. Be unreasonable today. Be open. Be
present. Be patient. And do not tell yourself any stories about what you
think is possible. Just remind yourself frequently that with God, lots
can happen . . . and the how and when is none of your business. Your
job is to hold the mystical space for Light to flow through today.

85

You Can Make It Happen, But You Can't Make It Work

o o o o o o o o o o o o o o o o o o o o o o o o o o o o o o o o o

Today we will receive instead of plan, that we may give instead of organize . . . if there are plans to make, you will be told of them. They may not be the plans you thought were needed, nor indeed the answers to the problems which you thought confronted you.

-A Course in Miracles

If something is part of the divine plan for your life, you can make all kinds of mistakes and things will still continue to unfold in a nearly effortless manner. If it is not part of the divine plan, you can do everything absolutely perfectly and things will still continue to fall apart in an atmosphere of struggle and efforting.

You cannot make anyone love you and you cannot earn love no matter how perfectly you do everything or how much you give. None of your strategies will really work - you may attain form, but the content will simply not be there if it is not part of the divine unfolding of your life. And if someone does love you, you may make an enormous amount of mistakes and act in a truly unworthy manner over and over again . . . and still, there they are loving you. Your part is to do your best FOR YOUR OWN SAKE, not to get or keep anyone or anything.

Giving and receiving are the polar opposites of paying and getting. Paying and getting require strategizing, planning and organizing. Giving and receiving are natural and spontaneous, like breathing in and out . . . no thought or strategies required. Trying to earn love, respect, acknowledgment and approval are exhausting and do not work. Replaying the scenes over and over to see how you could have done it differently or more perfectly to make it happen or make it work is a terrible kind of self-torture.

Anything that is truly yours by divine inheritance can never be taken away. People and situations are ALL temporary loaners for this physical incarnation and some stay longer than others. What is yours forever is the content, the lessons learned, the love given and received.

Let go of trying to make anything happen and instead let Life show you what is already working, what is already yours . . . and practice remaining open to receive whatever is next.

86

Do It Fat

Delay does not matter in eternity, but it is tragic in time.

-A Course in Miracles

You life is now. Patience and learning how to wait with a good attitude are major lessons in growth for every miracle worker, but there are other times and situations in which the ego counsels waiting so that you will not participate fully in your joyful mission. It wants you to miss your experience of life.

Waiting to go swimming because you feel too fat to go to the beach, waiting for the exact right circumstances before you will take a dance class, waiting for the children to be fully grown and out of the house before you take care of yourself at all, waiting for circumstances to align in some mythical way so that you will be totally assured of complete success or of not appearing foolish in any way - these are merely delay tactics of the ego.

We would not have you taking foolish risks or being totally irresponsible of course. There is no reason to plunge yourself into unnnecessary debt when it is wiser for you to save up the money to pay cash for something. You don't need to put your physical health at risk by doing something that is far beyond what you are currently capable of - no need to try to do a marathon when you haven't even walked to the mailbox for a year!

However, there is much that you can do right now if you would just take one step beyond the ego's arbitrary limitations. This is not about busting out of your fear or hurling yourself into something terrifying - but, you can begin by taking small consistent steps beyond your self-made boundaries. You can take a penguin step today and then another and then another and see where it gets you. It takes penguins a looooong way.

Yes, We're saying that in some cases it's best to "do it fat, do it old, do it broke, do it clumsy, do it embarrassed, do it young, do it sick." Stop stopping yourself all the time. Ask for Our Guidance on whether whatever you are considering doing is part of the Divine Will for you and We will let you know. And if you ask for Our Help . . . well, that is Our greatest pleasure in the whole Universe.

87

Do Not Let the Ego Steal Your JOY

o o o o o o o o o o o o o o o o o o o o o o o o o o o o o o o o

There is no need to learn through pain. And gentle lessons are acquired joyously, and are remembered gladly.

-A Course in Miracles

The Holy Spirit is a gentle Teacher whose purpose IS your joy and happiness. The ego thought system will always try to pervert those gentle lessons so that you will become more defensive, wounded and bitter. These things steal away your joy and leave you prey to your own fearful thinking and projections.

You CAN decide otherwise. When Jesus said, "get thee behind me Satan" it was a direct order to that ego thought system to vacate His mind. You have the very same authority, but you only know this if you exercise it.

Sorry ego, I'm not going to let you steal my joy today.

I am choosing to let go of my pain, to forgive the unforgivable, to release resentments.

I am choosing to walk in Divine Love today.

I am choosing to believe the best about myself and about all others I see.

I am choosing to laugh and smile and suck the juice out of this day no matter what.

You have no power here.

Begone, before someone drops a house on you!

88

Consider This . . .

o o o o o o o o o o o o o o o o o o o o o o o o o o o o o o o

I do not perceive my own best interests.

-A Course in Miracles

Moses, Jesus, the Buddha, Lao Tzu, the greatest spiritual teachers of all time, none of them ever suggested that you make a list of what you want to "manifest" or create. None suggested a shopping list for the Universe to fulfill. Many mid-level and secondary entities and teachers DO suggest this because it is a mid-level secondary consciousness.

It is not wrong or bad to make such a list and it may even be fun for a while, particularly if it helps you to get it off your mind and onto the page. However, We suggest that if you do make such a list that you surrender it in prayer to the Holy Spirit and then put it in the paper shredder as an act of RELEASE.

Brother Jesus DID instruct you to ASK the great Father-Mother Creator for whatever you want but He also very wisely said, *"not my will, but Thy will be done."* And it is Our task to remind you that the Divine Will is always always good and always wise. Many of you want things that would not be good for you at all and that would not be good for those around you . . . but, you have no way of knowing that because there are too many variables that you are not privy to in life.

Ask for and receive your DAILY bread rather than asking for a lifetime of manna to come to you today.

If you want to practice the best kind of asking, ask for happiness, joy, peace and to be used for good purpose today. Life is so much simpler than you sometimes make it.

89

Line Up Your Energies

o o o o o o o o o o o o o o o o o o o o o o o o o o o o o o o o

Before you choose to do anything, ask me if your choice is in accord with mine. If you are sure that it is, there will be no fear.

-A Course in Miracles

Stop endlessly second-guessing yourself little miracle worker. So often you make a decision and then you mentally make that decision wrong and scatter your energies to the winds of doubt and fear. It would be so much better to line up behind your decision once it has been made, maintaining a willingness to be corrected, remembering that you can always change your mind.

If you have gone within and asked the Internal Teacher, that gut feeling of connected intuition and Universal Wisdom to guide you, then you will have all the Help you need along the way. Once you have asked for Guidance and have made the decision based on that, line up behind that decision. Let the gut lead and then bring the mind and the heart into alignment behind it.

Now, if you "forgot" to ask for Divine Guidance to begin with and made the choice from a fearful perception, it is still not too late. Miracles can undo these misperceptions in the present. Close your eyes, take a deep breath, become still and go inside now. Ask for Help.

Ask to be gently guided and corrected if correction is necessary. Ask for a miracle.

> *It will never happen that you must make decisions for yourself.*
> *You are not bereft of help, and Help that knows the answer.*

-A Course in Miracles

90

Today's Prayer

God is with me now. He has a plan for my life.
I believe in the power of God. I believe in miracles.
I believe in the radical action of God's love here on Earth.
There is no opposite to this power -
it flows from God through me now.
All love and understanding fills my heart.
God uses my hands, my feet and my voice this day to do His will.
All good is effortlessly drawn to me today.
I cannot fail to be at the right place at the right time.
There is limitless good - more than enough for everyone.
There is no need to worry or rush, the Universe has perfect timing.
I embrace this new day and the miracles it brings.
I am a radiant beam of light which attracts friends,
love, success, good health and joy.
I am not afraid to be happy today. I am not afraid of love.
I am thankful for all this good and for my life.
I step back now and allow the Universe to do the work.
I do not interfere nor doubt.
I trust that it is done and so it is.
Amen

91

You Deserve to Live

o o o o o o o o o o o o o o o o o o o o o o o o o o o o o o o

Your worth is not established by teaching or learning. Your worth is established by God . . . Again - nothing you do or think or wish or make is necessary to establish your worth.

-A Course in Miracles

It is not necessary for you to earn the space you occupy on earth. Many of you spend your days working to somehow justify your mere existence. Again, this is the ego's curriculum of guilt at work. It is the exact opposite of the curriculum of Spirit.

Too often you leave out the "fun-factor" of the curriculum and take things far too seriously. Remember that We have need of JOYFUL teachers and not dour martyrs. You will be most useful to Us and to the Greater Plan if you will simply devote today to joyful teaching and learning. What is there to learn? Learn that the children of God are all essentially innocent. People may do horrible things because their thoughts are insane and twisted by fear, but their spiritual nature remains clean and pure. Teach them Who they are today by extending joy. And remember, that to teach is to demonstrate.

Let yourself off the hook today. As you focus on the innocence in yourself, it will be much easier to see it in others. This is your assignment today. Take it lightly and easily and know that it will be a lesson that will serve you well in increasing your happiness and usefulness.

92

Make a Better Choice

o o o o o o o o o o o o o o o o o o o o o o o o o o o o o o

*Trials are but lessons that you failed to learn presented once again,
so that where you made a faulty choice before you now can make
a better one, and thus escape all pain that what you chose before
has brought to you.*

-A Course in Miracles

This is what much of your life comes down to miracle worker - making
good choices. And how wonderful to know that you get more than one
opportunity to improve! When it feels like you are in a trial by fire, you
are never being punished - you are being given an opportunity to make
a better choice than you've made in the past. And it's not necessarily
that you made an altogether loveless choice in the past - however, there
is obviously room for further improvement here and sometimes the
best students do have more intense learning opportunities. Do not
resist the lessons before you.

How to do this though? With Help. Again, you cannot be your own
guide for miracles since it is your limited human mind that made them
necessary. It is the Presence of the Divine Mind within you, the Holy
Spirit or Internal Teacher Whom you must turn to in order to make
the better choice now.

Divine Mother - Help me to make the better choice today in all things.

*I surrender my judgments to you. Please heal my mind and open my
heart.*
I choose the Path of Light today and cannot find it on my own.
Lead on Your gentle paths as I humbly receive Your Guidance now. Amen

93

Ready, Willing and Able

○ ○

*As you share **My** inability to tolerate lack of love in yourself and others, you **must** join the Great Crusade to correct it. The slogan for the Crusade is "Listen, learn and do": **Listen** to My voice, **learn** to undo error, and **do** something to correct it. The power to work miracles belongs to you. I will provide the opportunities to do them, but you must be ready and willing since you are already able.*

-A Course in Miracles

We understand how frustrated you get with the state of lovelessness that dominates your world. We see how much anxiety, depression and anger it activates within you to push against seeming injustice and inequality. Your Spirit is inherently just and fair so you find it difficult to observe the projections of unfairness you see all around you.

The Christic Force within you cannot tolerate this lovelessness and that is why you came here - to be a part of the great correction of fear. It is the great Crusade to correct fear wherever you see it within yourself and others. You have been given gifts from God that will help you to make these corrections, but they must be Divinely Guided corrections and not the ones your ego mind tells you to make. You may not recognize what you true talents are, but as you learn to LISTEN to the Voice of God within you, you will be directed as to what to DO.

Delay no longer. Christ in you is ready now. What is required is your willingness to walk in love today. You are an Emissary of Light. Do not attack darkness or fear nor push against it- simply walk in Divine Love and leave a trail of Light as you go. Others will be blessed as they follow you, following Christ. Ask for Help often today and tune into the flow of energy. Your willingness is everything in this. You may not FEEL anything different or particularly "mystical" occurring - this is because miracles are natural and not something out of the ordinary. Trust that We know what We are doing through you even when you are totally unaware of the outcomes.

94

What Went Right

o o o o o o o o o o o o o o o o o o o o o o o o o o o o o o o o

This is a course in mind training. All learning involves attention and study at some level.

-A Course in Miracles

There is nothing easier than to focus your attention on what is wrong, what is not working, what is not satisfactory. It is completely debilitating and exhausting, yet it is much easier for many of you. Therefore, it takes a certain amount of training, attention and study to create the new habit of paying attention to the good, the beautiful and the holy. It takes more effort and sometimes you are a bit lazy about what you give your attention to so We are suggesting that you being a "What Went Right" journal or daily list. (it is not enough to do it in your head – PUT IT DOWN ON PAPER!!)

Perception is what gives your life meaning - the meaning YOU give it. For instance, so often when the form of a particular relationship ends, it is common for loved ones to look at it with disappointment and say, "So sorry it didn't work out." Well, the response to that is this, "It DID work out. THIS is how it worked out. It's not a disappointment or a failure. It worked out as another beautiful lesson in love and now life moves onto what is next."

It's only in a story of attachment to form and space and time that anything "doesn't work out." All that means is that the ego did not get what it wanted. But Spirit sees only the love given and the love received in every situation.

It takes discipline and consistency to keep up the work of shifting from the ego mind to the Christ mind, from the hungry ghosts to the heart of the Buddha. So, We urge you in every situation, and particularly those in which you are tempted to look at as a "failure" to make a list of What Went Right instead of allowing ego to effortlessly catalog its list of everything that it sees as awful, fearful, depressing and full of accusations of guilt and shame. Take charge of your mind to day by guiding it to what is going right in your life today. Acknowledge it, activate the feelings behind it and give endless thanks - the Universe will bring to you experiences that match that consciousness to prove you are right.

95

MEANING WELL – DOING RIGHT

o o o o o o o o o o o o o o o o o o o o o o o o o o o o o

*Trust not your good intentions. They are not enough. But trust
implicitly your willingness, whatever else may enter.*

-A Course in Miracles

Modern metaphysics has made quite a big thing about the power of
intention. But many people with good intentions live lives of chaos,
drama and negative passivity while they go along hurting themselves
and those around them. You see, love is an action, not a feeling. Do not
confuse affection and love. Real love is much more than an affectionate
feeling.

You may have all kinds of affectionate feelings toward a pet. You
may be quite well-meaning in your intentions towards her. But if you
do not actually do right by her with your actions of feeding her every
day, she could die from starvation. You may SAY "I love you" to her all
the time while you let her starve to death and she would much rather
have you do right by her than to simply mean well.

Many "good hearted" people lie and steal and cheat all the time
due to their addictions or other forms of emotional imbalances and
illnesses. People who profess their love and who DO have affectionate
feelings toward a loved one may still beat and abuse them. They may
INTEND to love and protect them, but they are DOING the exact

opposite. They may have a good heart, but a tormented mind which they are not seeking help in healing.

Others may not actually do wrong but they passively allow everything to fall apart around them because they don't want to upset anyone. In other words, meaning well is simply not enough. Good intentions are not enough. Your life will be the result of the seeds you sow through your actions - where you show up, what you actually DO - these are the causes that will set the law into motion in your life ALONG with your high intentions. They are meant to work together and not alone or separately.

Think of it this way, your bodily condition is mostly the effect of whether you are doing right by it, not what your intentions are. If you are thinking loving thoughts, taking good care of it, treating it with actual kindness, moving it, feeding it well, then it will respond to that. You can intend all kinds of things about your body and have many many good intentions - and good intentions are a wonderful start. But faith without works is dead. This is not about being legalistic or going for perfection or increasing guilt when you fall short in your actions. Remember it is progress, not perfection. Be kind to yourself as you grow into spiritual maturity and keep records of each little step forward that you make. Give yourself credit for showing up and making the effort even if it does not go well.

If you need help in taking positive action in your life, today is the day. This is the day to reach out and start to take the penguin steps forward that will lead you into the life you deserve. Start now. Don't wait another day. We will Help you. Pray for Help and then take the first step forward that your intuition guides you to. It is a process and even if the first step you make is not THE answer, it will lead you to the next step. Miracles will happen if you are willing to change.

96

The Mind's Natural Anti-Depressant

○ ○

*I do not need gratitude, but you need to develop your weakened ability to be grateful, or you cannot appreciate God. He does not need your appreciation, but **you** do.*

-A Course in Miracles

Gratitude is spitting in the eye of the ego. It's throwing a bucket of water on the wicked witch. Expressing gratitude is not for the other person's sake - it is for YOUR sake. It is impossible to be grateful and depressed simultaneously. But you cannot just spout the words of gratitude, you must actually allow the FEELING of gratitude to envelop you. Mindlessly making a gratitude list each day will not do you any good unless you actually invoke the FEELING of gratitude to well up within you as you make the list. Take your time. BE grateful and BE gratitude itself. Gratitude is an end in itself and you need to practice feeling grateful because of all the enormous benefits to YOU.

If you never remembered any other spiritual practice in your life, gratitude would be enough.

97

Divine Intervention

o o o o o o o o o o o o o o o o o o o o o o o o o o o o o o

Your newborn purpose is nursed by angels, cherished by the Holy Spirit and protected by God Himself.

-A Course in Miracles

There are times when nothing that you can say or do will get through to someone. At these times your attempts to break through often only make matters worse. When you reach this point, it is time to turn to the angels to deliver your communications.

You can always write a letter to the angel of any of your earthly brothers or sisters. Each of you has a guardian angel with you and it is quite simple to write a letter to the angel of your friend. You can do this to make amends when they are not ready to hear your apology, you can do this to ask for intervention, you can do this to ask for forgiveness, to extend forgiveness, or to say whatever it is that you need to say.

Many many miracles have come from this process and doors that have been long blocked have opened after this sacred communication has been made. But mostly, it has created release and peace in the one doing the writing. This is sowing a seed of faith and it can reap a divine harvest.

98

Instant Peace

○ ○

Seek not to change the world but choose to change your mind about the world.

-A Course in Miracles

So many are trying desperately to get a bigger piece of the garden without fully honoring or taking care of the corner they already have.

You can spend all your energy trying to get what you want so that you can be happy - or you can simply shift your focus and want what you have now. Instant peace.

99

The Path of Least Resistance

o o o o o o o o o o o o o o o o o o o o o o o o o o o o o o o

And if you find resistance is strong and dedication weak, you are not ready. Do not fight yourself. But think about the kind of day you want, and tell yourself there is a way in which this very day can happen just like that.

-A Course in Miracles

The ego loves the idea of "making things happen" and conquering situations and even self. This is a high-anxiety, high-stress path. Remember that the Tao does nothing and yet everything is done. This is one of the paradoxes of the spiritual life and Brother Jesus spoke of them often.

It seems irresponsible to the carnal mind to relax and trust that a Greater Power can handle the details of your life and therefore the path of least resistance appears lazy and unambitious. But let Us remind you that divine thinking is 180 degrees away from the thinking of the world. When you fight against something you merely give it your power and it grows stronger.

Whipping yourself, your world and the people around you into shape is endless and hopeless. Rise above the battleground today, end the war within, walk away from the fight and instead become the Visionary that you are. Remind yourself that what you really want is a day of happiness and peace and that the way to this goal is not to make it happen, but to get out of the way and let it happen.

100

Relationships: Graduate School Level

You will find many opportunities to blame your brother for the "failure" of your relationship, for it will seem at times to have no purpose. A sense of aimlessness will come to haunt you, and to remind you of all the ways you once sought for satisfaction and thought you found it. Forget not now the misery you really found, and do not breathe life into your failing ego. For your relationship has not been disrupted. It has been saved.

-A Course in Miracles

Remember that relationships are assignments and are the most important part of this particular curriculum. The ego becomes more frantic and agitated over this area of your earth experience than any other because it focuses relationships entirely on the body and cares nothing about what is real and eternal. This is why you so often experience relationships as a kind of living crucifixion. The ego focuses on form and not on content and this is a very fearful perception.

In Truth, all relationships are purposeful and none are more important than any other. Each one has the potential to take you to heaven or to hell, depending upon whom you choose as your internal guide. Again, the important thing to remember is that **you do not**

know. You think you know what purpose someone has in your life and the ego becomes enraged if they fail to fulfill the role you have assigned to them. But the Holy Spirit knows that there is only one purpose to every relationship - to restore both of you to the awareness of your inherent innocence. This is true in romance, business, families and even in your relationship to your own body which you have assigned a role to fulfill.

Today, try to see every person in your life as a divine assignment in which the only purpose is to extend love, rather than to try to manipulate the form. Be present. Breathe. Relax. Stay open. Let go of the purpose you had for it and instead, allow its true gifts to reveal themselves to you. We have waited this long to begin this part of your curriculum because We know how touchy you get around the subject. We have much to teach you - try not to freak out.

101

Lighten the Fuck Up

o o o o o o o o o o o o o o o o o o o o o o o o o o o o o o o o o

Into eternity, where all is one, there crept a tiny, mad idea, at which the Son of God remembered not to laugh.

-A Course in Miracles

How's your fun factor lately miracle worker? Are you taking yourself too seriously again? Worry and anxiety are a sure sign that you've gotten significant again and have forgotten that *"to heal is to make happy."*

Try to remember that no "body" makes it out of here alive but YOU are eternal. This is merely another cosmic temp assignment so why get so attached to your cubicle and desk? Nothing here lasts and yet it is all here for you to use and enjoy. Relax and make the best of each experience as it comes. Serious healers, serious relationships, serious careers - these are egoic intentions and they make you crazy and hard to get along with. Not only that, they actually INTERFERE with the natural joyous unfolding of your assignment here.

Happy healers, playful relationships, joyous careers - this is God's will for you and your part is simply to show up without attachment to the specifics. Stop trying to EARN your way into salvation, it is a GIFT that has already been given. Instead, be a happy light-hearted receiver and conduit for all that you've been given to use today. If you are living sanely today, tomorrow will take care of itself.

102

Give People a Fucking Break

o o o o o o o o o o o o o o o o o o o o o o o o o o o o o o

Your brother who stands beside you seems to be a stranger. You do not know him and your interpretation of him is very fearful. And you attack him still, to keep what seems to be yourself unharmed. Yet in his hands is your salvation. You see his madness, which you hate because you share it.

-A Course in Miracles

Jesus said to the crowd about the adulterous woman, "Whoever is without sin, cast the first stone." He did not say, "Whoever has not also committed **adultery**, cast the first stone." The message there is, you may not have done what **she** did, but you HAVE done some pretty stupid shit along the way. And it is your disowned guilt that you now project onto someone else in order to not feel it in yourself. You project it outward onto another person, and then feel justified in attacking them because of it. You hate the madness that you share and so you deny that you have it at all. You do not realize you are rejecting yourself and guaranteeing a sense of separation and despair.

The immature miracle worker loves to recognize their own evolution along the path, but are often not so willing to believe that others may be evolving too. Remember that guilt is the ego's orgasm. It is never so ecstatic as when it finds guilt in someone else. The mature miracle worker understands that true charity is assuming the best about others. His Course says, *"Charity is a way of looking at another as if he had already gone far beyond his actual accomplishments in time."*

Is your past completely impeccable? Would every decision you've ever made and everything you've ever said look brilliant if posted in the newspaper today? Have you NEVER said or even THOUGHT anything racist, sexist, ageist or homophobic? Were you a 9 year old totally evolved and enlightened being? Hardly. And it's doubtful you were all that evolved at 20 or 30.

This is an excellent day to practice charity. Assume the best about others even when they don't seem to be actualizing it yet. Many of you are far too worried about your financial investments when it is your investment in humanity that needs much more of your attention. You're a miracle worker. Act like it today.

103

Don't Just Talk About Prayer. Pray!

o o o o o o o o o o o o o o o o o o o o o o o o o o o o o o o

Prayer is the medium of miracles.

-A Course in Miracles

You may believe in prayer. You may profess the benefits of prayer. You may have a great deal of faith in prayer. But, are you praying and how often? Not prayer to some mythical God outside of you up in the sky on a cloud asking for special favors and to have the details of your life fixed but, true prayer of aligning with the Infinite Creative Source for your greatest good. We are talking about affirmative prayer here.

To "pray without ceasing" is a given. You are already praying without ceasing in a sense because your thoughts are always so active. But are they prayers of faith and love or prayers of worry and fear?

Begin DIRECTING your faith with more constancy now little miracle worker. Start by making this a day of prayer - and then a week of prayer - a month of prayer and stretch it out as far as you can. You don't need to face anything alone, ever.

104

I See Only Perfection Today

o o o o o o o o o o o o o o o o o o o o o o o o o o o o o o o o

I am responsible for what I see.

-A Course in Miracles

Your mind projects meaning on everything your eyes look upon and because of this, you are responsible for what you see. Your eyes fall on a homeless person and then goes into its story about homeless people. Your eyes fall upon your bank balance and then mind goes into a story about what it has decided that means. But these are only stories and they are either happy stories you tell yourself or they are horror shows that you repeat. They bring up fear or compassion, kindness or revulsion, terror or serenity - all based on your own projections. It is up to you. You are the interpreter of whatever you see.

Decide to see only perfection today and if your commitment is strong, mind will prove you right. If you don't like the story, drop it or tell a better version. Let Us remind you again to never let the ego steal your joy. All that you see around you is either love or a call for love. So if you look and do not see love, know that it is because YOU are the one assigned to project love onto the scene. This is what miracle workers do. It is a great and wonderful way to go through life!

105

Less Pathology, More Mythology

○ ○

No evidence will convince you of the truth of what you do not want.

-A Course in Miracles

Your western cultures love to pathologize everything and most of you are too well aware of all the possible syndromes you may have. You are all arm chair psychotherapists and diagnose yourselves based on things you see on the television and your answers to most problems is to medicate it away. In fact, many of you love to identify yourselves by your illnesses, wounds and disorders. You use "facts," figures, studies and statistics to paralyze yourselves into hopelessness and despair.

Once again, extremes are the ego's answer to everything because it puts you in a box of suffering. We teach the Buddha's "middle way" path of balance and harmony. When one has gone too far into the western pathologizing of self, it can be very helpful to return to the miraculous and to move into the 'dreamtime' again. Many of your problems you could just as well dance away as medicate away. Western medicine can be very helpful when it is balanced out with other more holistic remedies and practices so this is not about throwing out all your pills today. It is about adding something else.

Growing numbers of people go off every summer to the desert for a week-long community experience which ends with a fire ritual as a way of bringing mythology and mysticism back into their lives again. It is less of a tribe and more of a creation of a personal myth for each person and group who attends. The psyche is allowed to find necessary expression and regains balance through costumes and dance and creating gifts in a way that it does not usually do in your modern cities. It is the same reason that Halloween becomes more and more a holiday which adults celebrate.

Our desire is that you bring the mystical and mythological back into your day-to-day experiences to balance out the technological aspects of your life. Miracles are daily occurrences for an open heart and mind. They are normal and natural but they simply will not be seen by a buttoned-down mind. Break out of your daily uniform from time to time and add a bit of costuming here and there - a sparkle, a feather, a scent. Look for the fairies in the garden. Start gathering up evidence of miracles in the modern world. Talk to the Great Spirit of the mountain, the tree and the wind. Be bold. Be free. Be weird. It's so much more fun that way.

106

The Gratitude Experiment

o o o o o o o o o o o o o o o o o o o o o o o o o o o o o o o o o

What is Heaven but a song of gratitude and love and praise by everything created to the Source of its creation?

-A Course in Miracles

Here's a simple little faith-building practice to put in your spiritual toolbox. It's the 30 Day Gratitude Experiment and it's very easy to do.

Just choose something that's been worrying you, on your mind, or where you feel stuck and begin to give thanks that Spirit is taking care of it for you. Come from the mindset that it's already done. Do this as many times a day as the situations occurs to you. If you are alone, do it out loud and in fact it is much more powerful to speak the words out loud frequently throughout the day:

Thank You Divine Spirit for healing this for me!

And you can name the specifics if you want: *"healing this relationship - this illness - increasing my energy - bringing in the perfect resources, etc."*

Do this practice for 30 days and be open to acting on any guidance or direction you may receive during that time, but do not strategize or plan on your own. We are building your conviction through demonstration.

107

Healing and Wholeness

o o o o o o o o o o o o o o o o o o o o o o o o o o o o o o o o

If you are not a body, what are you? Ask this in honesty, and then devote several minutes to allowing your mistaken thoughts about your attributes to be corrected, and their opposites to take their place. Say, for example: I am not weak, but strong. I am not helpless, but all powerful. I am not limited, but unlimited. I am not doubtful, but certain. I am not an illusion, but a reality. I cannot see in darkness, but in light.

-A Course in Miracles

There is no need for you to fight against illness or any bodily conditions. You can merely neutralize them by withdrawing your faith in them and aligning yourself with Truth again. It is much more beneficial to stimulate the forces of healing than to fight against their opposites.

Realize the greater Truth about you and neutralize their opposites with positive denial. There is positive and negative denial. In negative denial you do not want to face something that disturbs you so you try to pretend it isn't there. This actually gives MORE of you attention to it because it take tremendous effort to keep pushing it down.

Positive denial is looking right at the situation and negating the frightening story you've told about it. Positive denial neutralizes the fear by stripping it of its power over you. Always follow up positive denial with affirming a deeper truth. AND you can still take medicine, or use any other medical means even while you are using your affirmations!

108

People Are Annoying

○ ○

You are not misguided; you have accepted no guide at all.

-A Course in Miracles

We are not here to lie to you or "blow smoke up your ass." The simple fact is, people are annoying and life in the body is extremely challenging. It's challenging and difficult for everyone because everyone has a mind that judges and evaluates. It's rather clear that even Brother Jesus got testy with people from time to time and particularly with the apostles - because of their annoying nature. He had His challenging relationships just as all people do.

As He put it to them then, where is the nobility or spirituality in loving people who are always lovable? Being nice to infants, kittens and puppies or to people who agree with all your opinions doesn't make one a spiritually mature being of great character. If you love plants, oceans, nature and animals but hate people, you still have a long long way to go on this journey.

It's when things are not to your liking that the rubber hits the road miracle worker. And We are here to constantly remind you that you are not expected to do any of this on your own. Miracles do not transform "unlovable" people into kind warm east-to-get-along-with folks. Miracles transform the mind of the miracle worker to see people differently. Jesus, Buddha, the Divine Mother, the Holy Spirit and a whole host of enlightened beings are available to be your Guide to miracles and to seeing correctly. To see correctly is to see with compassion, kindness and love.

Learn to ask for Help more in your seeing than in the conditions before you. Don't try to force yourself to see the good in something or someone - ask God to reveal it to you as you offer your willingness to be changed. Practice letting go of being right today and approach the day with innocence as you seek Divine Guidance in all your perceptions. Miracles WILL happen.

109

They Want to Know What You Want

Let us resolve today to ask for what we really want, and only this, that we may spend this day in fearlessness, without confusing pain with joy, or fear with love.

-A Course in Miracles

Many many times you think you know what you want and need, when in reality you are still a bit confused because you are going for the form rather than the content. But, this does not mean that you should not ask for certain forms if you really feel that is your need at the time. Mostly it it a process of becoming clear over time. Be patient with yourself and remember how many times when that moment of true clarity came, things happened very fast from that moment on.

There are Angels and Spirits all around ready to bring into your experience what you REALLY want rather than what you think you want. And if you just practice asking, asking, asking with a calm open non-attached mind, you will be a witness to your own beautifully unfolding life. More and more you will have the experience of effortless accomplishment of your aspirations.

So it's fine to make your lists as part of the process of clarifying within yourself - perhaps about where you want to live, the kind of job you'd like to do, the situations you'd like to experience in life. Just be careful that you don't make the mistake of thinking that your happiness lies there or that without these you will be a miserable failure. The co-creation game is meant to be great fun and the moment that you are not feeling joyful in it, you have taken over and are trying to force things again.

Remember, the Universe is a friendly place and wants to know what you want, not as a delivery system of your endless ego needs but in order to help you along the path to discovering your divine destiny. You won't get everything you want and for this you should be very glad. But keep asking as a grateful happy child asks a parent for it's earthly needs to be met. Every parent wants to do what is best for their child and the Divine Parents are no different. Ask away and then leave the final decision to Their infinite Wisdom.

110

Physical Healing

Physical Healing

There is a Divine Physician within me.
Eternal wisdom and healing abide in me.
I place my body in the care of the Supreme Intelligence.
This Intelligence is in every living thing that exists
and It exists in me now.
It perfectly runs my body and knows what to do and how to do it.
This Intelligence is the same power that Jesus
used to heal the sick and the dead.
I call on that Power to make Itself known in me.
Right now Divine Love is coursing through my veins and into my
organs and into every cell of my body.
Every breath I take relaxes my muscles, eases all tension
and leaves my mind peaceful and still.
There is nothing to strive for nor fight against - nothing to battle.
Whatever is happening in this body is loved and accepted for
anything that is not a reflection of Divine Love is temporary.
I love and bless this body just as it is and just as it is not.
It is a temporary vehicle and
I appreciate every detail the Creator made.
I allow myself to enjoy healthy foods and exercise as best I can.
I allow myself to be fully alive no matter
what the condition of my body.
I do not use my body for safety nor to hide.

This body is free of all my past emotions
and thoughts that were not of love.
I release any addictions or disorders for they have no power
in the presence of the Light.
Only the laws of God apply to my health.
I forgive myself for any harm
I may have done to my body in the past.
It is over now and can have no effect.
I identify myself with Spirit and not with the flesh.
I give thanks to my body for all that is had done for me.
I give thanks to God for healing it now.
All is well.

111

Restful Sleep

<u>Bedtime Prayer</u>

The Divine Mother Father Presence of God
now enters my consciousness as I let go of the day.
I let go of all that went wrong and all that went right.
I now recognize my mistakes and
release them into Divine Forgiveness.
I humbly accept the lessons learned.
I let go of those who may have hurt or offended me.
I will not take my anger to bed and so I let it all go now.
I am thankful for the blessings of this day and
for all the wonderful ways in which I have known love.
I am thankful to have been here another day.
As I sleep, my family and loved ones are
all held perfectly in the hands of God.
My sleep is restful and healing.
My mind and body relax and let go.
My dreams are peaceful and I receive any needed Guidance.
I invite the Angels to now enter my mind that they may
guide me to the higher realms of consciousness.
My home and all who abide here are filled with
Divine Love which protects us from any harm.
All are safe in Divine Care this night.
As I turn my eyes away from the outer world
I am filled with the assurance that God is in control.
May my sleep give me the rest I need that
tomorrow I may do better and be more open to love.
May I be made into the person that I was created to be.
For this I am so grateful.

112

Just Relax

o o o o o o o o o o o o o o o o o o o o o o o o o o o o o

The body is in need of no defense. This cannot be too often emphasized. It will be strong and healthy if the mind does not abuse it by assigning to it roles it cannot fill, to purposes beyond its scope, and to exalted aims which it cannot accomplish.

-A Course in Miracles

It is the ego's main manipulative tool of suffering to keep you body-identified rather than Spirit identified. When you say "I" you are almost always referring to some aspect of body-identification. It is this that allows fear to motivate you as you constantly try to protect the body and protect your self-concept.

If you can practice, even a few moments a day, sitting quietly in relaxation releasing all thoughts and worries about the body (what to feed it, how to house it, worries about old age or illness, how to use it to attract what you think you need) you will be taking a major step toward true liberation. In time you will find that balance has been achieved through following the Guidance received during these times of true rest.

So many of you have such hatred and fear of your own body and there is simply no good reason for it. The Holy Spirit sees the body as a means of communication only. If you can begin to practice this you will begin to see it with love and kindness. Even a body in a wheelchair that cannot move can communicate love through thought. Think loving thoughts about your body whatever it is experiencing today. Give it compassion, kindness and don't make so much of it. It is not who you are or even where you are. Who you are can never be contained by a body.

113

"Lady, it's your dream."

o o o o o o o o o o o o o o o o o o o o o o o o o o o o o

. . . you have caused the dream, and can accept another dream as well. But for this change in content of the dream, it must be realized that it is you who dreamed the dreaming that you do not like. It is but an effect that you have caused, and you would not be cause of this effect.

-A Course in Miracles

A woman is having a dream in which a hideous slimy monster is chasing her and eventually traps her down a dead-end alley. She is breathless, terrified and frozen with fear as she pleads with the monster, *"What are you going to do to me?!!"*

The monster calmly leans in and replies, *"I don't know lady, it's your dream."*

All that you see around you is merely the great illusion of mind projecting itself outward. Some spiritual traditions call it "maya" but We tend to simply call it, "the dream." Very few awaken from the dream all at once but instead move through stages from nightmare to an ever increasingly happier more joyful dream. This is the perceptual shift from fear to love and that is what the Course is all about - attaining inner-peace through this healing of perceptions.

But it begins with personal responsibility. At some point you begin to realize that YOU are the dreamer of the dream. God will not come in and save you from your illusions but has sent the Holy Spirit as a Guide to help you reinterpret all that you see as fearful and lead you to love.

You can dream a better dream. It happens one thought at a time, one perception at a time, one choice at a time. Do not ask that the images before you be changed. Ask instead that your thoughts be set right and you will begin to see the entire world differently.

114

No Bitching, No Whining

o o o o o o o o o o o o o o o o o o o o o o o o o o o o o o o

How sharper than a serpent's tooth it is to have a thankless child.

-King Lear, William Shakespeare

You so underestimate the power of your own thoughts and words. You seem to think that you can get away with minor but consistent chipping away at things without it having any adverse affect. This is ridiculous. Even something as gentle as water can wear away rock given enough time.

So much of your attention often goes to what is missing or not here yet or on what you wish were not here, and so little of your attention goes toward gratitude for what IS present. Do not again make the mistake of not knowing what you've got til it's gone. So many people wish they had back the body they judged 10 years ago. And 10 years from now those same people will wish they had the body they are now judging. We are shocked at the words that humans speak to their spouses, their "beloved" on a daily basis - words that belittle and criticize and break down the spirit of another person. Then they are shocked to find their mate has been having an affair with someone who appreciates them as they are. Millions are losing jobs they grumbled and murmured about on a daily basis. And even more crippling is the self-talk that goes on inside the minds of the mass of people on the earth each day!

Remember that gratitude is a major major fucking major part of the positive creative process. Did We drive that home enough? Very little is more powerful than a grateful attitude. Saying, *"I am really grateful but . . ."* is NOT gratitude. It is the introduction to a complaint.

If there is something in your life that you do not like, begin blessing it right now exactly as it is. Make lists of what is positive about it no matter how far you have to reach to find something. Begin to be so full of praise that people dread seeing you coming with your ridiculous positive attitude. Soon you will find just how powerful you are as your words begin to invoke the very best that life has to offer.

115

I'm Onto You!

o o o o o o o o o o o o o o o o o o o o o o o o o o o o o o o o o

We said before that the ego vacillates between suspiciousness and viciousness. It remains suspicious as long as you despair of yourself. It shifts to viciousness when you decide not to tolerate self-abasement and seek relief. Then it offers you the illusion of attack as a "solution."

-A Course in Miracles

Anytime that you find yourself feeling unworthy, unlovable, stupid, guilty and shameful simply look in the mirror and say, *"Look, I'm onto you! I know what you're trying to do ego and I'm not signing up for this trip to hell again so you might just as well give up now. I am 100% committed to focusing on love and acceptance today - no matter what!"* Be very very firm in this and know that the power of Divine Love in you can overcome any darkness or fear.

But also be aware that after you do this, the ego may get agitated because you are no longer tolerating the old self-hatred and it will try to get you to focus on the guilt in others instead. When this occurs, instead of simply loving and forgiving yourself, you begin to mentally attack others for "causing" your experience of low self-esteem or failure in life, etc. You begin seeking the guilty person or organization or social structure that you can blame it on. The ego doesn't really care who or what is being attacked. It doesn't matter to ego if it is yourself or another person. All it wants to do is destroy peace and joy in this moment by producing attack thoughts.

This is when it is so important to surrender to Spirit. You cannot fight the ego because by fighting against it you actually give it your power. The only win is to give up the battle entirely and turn to the Source of all life. Remember the ego is an illusion. It doesn't even exist - it is merely the word given to a fear-based thought system. There is no point going to war with an illusion now is there? Instead, turn to God-within and ask that your mind be healed and awakened to the truth.

This is one of those times when there are two of Our lists that will be of great benefit again:

Where I Got It Right - make a list of everything in the past 24 hours or the past week or month where you feel you showed up in a positive way for yourself, your life or another person.

Where They Got It Right - whoever your ego is trying to judge, attack and condemn - make a list of their positive aspects and any way in which you can see that they are trying and/or are showing up too.

116

Don't Should On Yourself (or anyone else)

○ ○

Guilt is a sure sign that your thinking is unnatural.

-A Course in Miracles

There is a healthy kind of remorse that arises whenever you react lovelessly to one of God's creations, including yourself. Most of you feel this healthy remorse when you react out of fear and say or do something loveless to another person or to yourself. It is an aid in recognizing when you have made a mistake so that you can ask for Help in correcting the error. There is no need for guilt or shame. Mistakes call for correction, not punishment.

However, too often you experience a harmful guilt which you either feel yourself or project onto others and it is usually tied up to the concept of "should" and "shouldn't" which is based entirely on judgments of the ego mind.

We are really not proponents of eliminating certain words from your vocabulary because it usually adds an unnecessary emphasis and actually creates MORE guilt. However, we are suggesting that you begin to notice the daily "shoulds and shouldn'ts" that arise in you. Just notice them without judgment. One way to do this is to take just one week of making a daily list of the the shoulds and shouldn'ts that you are carrying in your mind. If you do this with the correct attitude it will become extremely funny to you how long, impossible and hopeless this list is for yourself and for all the other people whom you think should or shouldn't be or do this or that.

ex: people should let me into traffic, Bob should always hang up his clothes, I should eat more vegetables, my mother should always acknowledge me, my children should thank me for all that I do for them, the government should do what I want them to, other people should vote the same way I do, my body shouldn't have wrinkles, I should have more energy, my mate should know what I want without me telling her, and on and on and on.

If you take this far enough each day you'll see how debilitating and unnecessary all of this is and you may begin to see that you are making life much much harder than it needs to be. As you let go of the shoulds your guilt will naturally begin to dissipate.

117

Invoking Chi

All healing is essentially the release from fear.

-A Course in Miracles

Relax miracle worker. This is Our primary message when it comes to healing of any kind. You cannot make yourself well but you can certainly make your body ill.

Physical healing is not about making yourself well but rather is getting out of the way to allow the obstructions to wholeness begin to fall away. It is already built into the system for the body to regulate itself perfectly. When there is imbalance, all of the cells begin automatically invoking Chi restoration and this can be experienced as all kinds of physical sensations. Try not to be alarmed or resistant. Instead, become more still and relaxed. Go inside and listen with kindness.

Whether you use Eastern tonics, Western medicine, prayer, yoga, or any particular modality is not the point here. The point is to use whatever is helpful to YOU in decreasing fear and increasing inner-peace. Remember that this is a highly individualized curriculum and what works for one may not work for all when it comes to the forms of healing. But in the end, for true healing to take place, there must be a release from fear.

So whatever may be going on in your body, remember that it is your thoughts about it that will either create fear or compassion within you. Ask for Spirit to guide your thoughts and to lead you to whatever will allow you to relax enough to let the Chi restore balance and harmony. Let go of time and how long it may or may not take. Use whatever means you are guided to use which create more calm within you and do not think one is more "spiritual" than another. There is only what is right for you in this moment. Relax. Breathe. Do not fight against any condition but instead continue knowing that a dynamic action is taking place within you as all things are held perfectly in the hands of God. And whatever sensations you are experiencing in your body, remind yourself that the body is calling forth what it needs to restore all things to perfect order again.

118

Calling Forth the Light

o o o o o o o o o o o o o o o o o o o o o o o o o o o o o o

When a brother behaves insanely, you can heal him only by perceiving the sanity in him.

-A Course in Miracles

To invoke is to call something forth that is already present but not yet seen. To be a miracle worker you must practice practice practice letting go of your tendency to judge according to appearances. Appearances are just the surface and are often illusory anyhow. We are asking you to look beyond them to a deeper realm.

Just because someone is not demonstrating their more divine qualities does not mean they do not have them. They are present in everyone and if you want to see them in one who is not demonstrating them, you must invoke them. When someone is behaving in an unloving manner, you only make it worse as you focus on their behavior. You actually affirm their fear and lock it into place. The more you focus on it the stronger it will become.

We are not asking you to pretend or deny or cover over anything - but We are asking you to affirm and call forth their better angels. You can do this silently within yourself or you can do it verbally by beginning to acknowledge whatever good you can find within them. You may not realize it but you are almost constantly calling forth energies and qualities from people and from situations. You can do this consciously and deliberately or you can do it unconsciously and by default. Their is tremendous power in focus.

And if you want to see a truly miraculous shift, verbally acknowledge something wonderful within whomever you see as a problem and watch how they seem to magically match exactly what you acknowledged even if it is a quality they have never demonstrated before in their entire lives. Dour people can become funny. Crabby people can become charming. Selfish people can become generous. All through the power of invocation.

119

You Can Afford to Relax

o o o o o o o o o o o o o o o o o o o o o o o o o o o o o o o

*And what we think is weakness can be strength; what we believe
to be our strength is often arrogance.*

-A Course in Miracles

This is what We really want you to see and understand. In fact, when
you don't relax you are actually interfering with the natural process
of your unfolding good. We will be repeating this lesson frequently
from this point on so that you can begin to experience how deep it
goes.

Things fit, or they don't. They work, or they don't. Someone likes
you, or they don't. The door is open, or it's closed. The lights are green,
or they're red. And chasing after something that does not want you is
usually extremely painful and stressful.

When you relax and let go, it doesn't mean that you don't care,
stop showing up or become negatively passive. It simply means you
can read the signs and you stop arguing with them. There is always
an open door for you and you will see it if you remain relaxed yet
awake.

Show up. Show up on time. Show up prepared. Let the rest go. You are not in charge of the Universe. Be glad. It would be far too stressful.

Remember, Our goal is not conquest - it's inner-peace. And inner-peace is the beginning of a life of incredible joy, love and abundance of good.

120

Don't Give Up – Just Let Go

o o o o o o o o o o o o o o o o o o o o o o o o o o o o o o o

You find it difficult to accept the idea that you need give so little, to receive so much. And it is very hard for you to realize it is not personally insulting that your contribution and the Holy Spirit's are so extremely disproportionate . . . if you believe the holy instant is difficult for you, it is because you have become the arbiter of what is possible, and remain unwilling to give place to One Who knows.

-A Course in Miracles

Let God be God. It's just so much easier that way. Do your little part and let the rest go. To "give up" is to walk away in despair, anger, frustration and hopelessness. To "let go" is to step back and surrender to a Force greater than your own self-will.

How simple is it to put a little seed in the ground, water it and step back while it grows into a fruit tree which gives abundant fruit for many generations to come? How disproportionate is your part to what the Universe then provides from that small action. Of yourself, you could never "make" an apple, an orange or a peach. It is done through a perfectly natural process which you can cooperate with or fight against. You cannot take personal credit for it. You've conquered nothing. You are not a hero even though your action may benefit thousands and thousands whom you will never meet or hear of through the fruit of this tree.

Your life is just like that tree miracle worker. You cannot "make" it work or "make" it happen if it is against the natural divine order of your life. As you push and push against people, situations and self you simply exhaust yourself and move farther and farther from your own center. But you can let go of that struggle and let the force of the Great Mother Tao carry you downstream. You have a small part to play in things going well, but it is quite small. And though it is very small, the harvest is tremendous.

There is certainly work to be done during harvest-time but again, compared to what the Natural Order has provided, it is still extremely small. Remember that you do not know what is possible. You do not know where the path will go next and have no proper criteria to judge it by. Being fired may lead you to a new fulfilling career. Getting "dumped" may lead you to a whole creative new chapter in your life. Losing your house may set you on a path to world travel. Being given a "terminal" diagnosis may set you on the road to a peace and joy that you never knew existed. Being humiliated publicly may turn you into a beacon of Light to millions who will hear your new message of humility and service.

Again, do your part, show up ready and on time and full of willingness to cooperate with the energies present at that moment. Stay present, open, humble, teachable and let the rest go. In other words, get the fuck out of the way.

121

Boot Camp Reminders

o o o o o o o o o o o o o o o o o o o o o o o o o o o o o o o o

You are far too tolerant of mind wandering and are passively condoning your minds miscreations.

-A Course in Miracles

Universal laws are ruthless and exacting and are no respecter of persons. If a baby crawls out of a 5th story window, gravity doesn't violate its own laws because the baby is an innocent who doesn't understand how life works. It is completely fair in that it works exactly the same for every living being. The sun shines on Jesus in the exact same way that it shines on Hitler.

A computer doesn't care that you have never used one before, have good intentions, are trying your best and are soooo CLOSE to hitting the right key. It will not respond until you do EXACTLY what it requires for proper response. It is also totally fair that way.

The laws of mind are the same. You will experience the EXACT feelings that match your thoughts regardless of your good intentions. You may intend to be happy, but if you do not deliberately focus your mind on the thoughts that stimulate happiness, then you are not complying with the mental laws of cause and effect. If you whine and grumble and complain, the law of compensation will fill you with feelings of depression, anger, loneliness and pain. If you praise, appreciate and positively acknowledge, the law of compensation will fill you with feelings of love, abundance, peace and connection to LIFE.

There are times when you have to go back to boot camp to get in metaphysical shape again. Don't get sloppy and lazy in your focus and thinking - but if and when you do, head back to boot camp until you're feeling strong and focused again. Boot camp is hard - it's not for whiners. If it's not hard, it's not boot camp. The drill sargent is not here to hold your hand and baby you. He's here to kick your ass until you are thinking and acting like a Jedi Knight. Remember, if you are thinking right in the present, the future takes care of itself.

122

Jiggle the Molecules

o o o o o o o o o o o o o o o o o o o o o o o o o o o o o o o o

Love and joy are the same thing.

-A Course in Miracles

Lotions and potions are all well and good as far as they go but there is nothing that stimulates vibrancy and health more than learning to cooperate with and even manage chi, your vital life energy. Many of you go around leaking energy all over the place, ignoring all the signs that your inner-Guidance system is giving you, powering through them thinking you cannot afford to stop and take care of yourself.

Of course the ego keeps you from realizing how extremely expensive it is to ignore those signs. It can cost you everything if it goes far enough, including the life of the body itself. How simple it is to learn to tune into your own chi and to work with it instead of against it. There is nothing complicated that you need to learn. Just listen. The body loves to move. It wants to move. The cells are calling for it at whatever level you are capable of today. And the more you move, the more you will be able to and the more you will enjoy it.

Our favorite is simply walking. But if and when you can, dance. One of your most famous actors of the last century called dancing, "jiggling the molecules" and We know this to be a totally accurate description of true dance. Music that encourages your joyful emotions will flood the cells of your body with LOVE itself. If you are in a wheelchair and the only thing you can move are your arms, move them to the music. The chi knows what to do and how to do it. Your part is joyful movement. The rest will take care of itself and you will find that there is an increase in vital energy.

Keep the mind and heart open and you will be guided to the movements that are best for you on any given day. Tai chi, yoga, walking, hiking, Qi Gong, swimming, dancing, running, sports - the forms are not what matters, the joy is the thing. Movement and joy are the miracle potion. Drink it in.

123

Expand Your Boundaries

o o o o o o o o o o o o o o o o o o o o o o o o o o o o o o o

Are you ready yet to help Me save the world?

-A Course in Miracles

Do you realize that God is not held back by any past precedent? The Universe is an ever-expanding organism that is not held back by what has come before. It is only YOU who seem to hold it back in your own individual experience by your limited ability to receive. THIS is the work friend, expanding your capacity to accept the blessings of God without excuse.

Your age, your past, your perceived defects and limitations, your neurosis, illnesses, and all of the mistakes of your past do not matter IF you are open to receive. It's just a yes or no question really - all the rest is just your story and justifications. The world will be saved from fear and attack by those who are willing to be the vessels for radical love and peace. It will be saved by people who the world may see as the worst possible choices, but the Great Architect deliberately chooses the stones that the builder has rejected to make the cornerstone of the Temple of Light.

Expand your self-imposed boundaries miracle worker. Dwell in possibilities today instead of what you think are the probabilities. Lots can happen that you are totally unaware of and could never imagine in a thousand years. The only thing that matters is whether your valve is open or closed today.

124

When You Believe

○ ○

If thou canst believe, all things are possible to him that believeth.

-Mark 9:23

Step out of the ordinary mindset of limitation today miracle worker. You have been trained to think unnaturally and We are working day and night to retrain your mind to its natural spaciousness. You have no idea the beauty that lies before you which we are actively planning and preparing you for as much as you will allow Us to.

Let God do a new thing in you by thinking a new thought. Look at it this way, if in all the history of humankind anyone has ever been healed, ever been made whole, ever been prospered, ever been lifted up, ever moved beyond their past limitations, ever had something unexpected and wonderful happen to them, why not you? Why not now?

There are NO special people. Only open minds or closed minds.

125

Only Love Heals

o o o o o o o o o o o o o o o o o o o o o o o o o o o o o o

Be not afraid of love. For it alone can heal all sorrow, wipe away all tears, and gently waken from his dream of pain the Son whom God acknowledges as His. Be not afraid of this.

-A Course in Miracles

You may think this a ridiculous quote. You may argue that you crave love and are not afraid of it at all. But then We must ask you why you try so cleverly to guard your heart? Why is it that you think that by holding back a little bit you somehow keep yourself safe? What are you saving it for? Love only grows and thrives as it circulates.

The time for holding back has passed miracle worker. You keep yourself safe from the miracle that would heal you. Your affirmations and energy treatments may "cure" a physical condition, but only love actually "heals" anything. The greatest healers of all time had little or no "technique" but had a deep, powerful and often non-attached love for those who came to them.

Yes it is true that you hunger for love, but the love that feeds and nourishes you is the love that you freely give and the love that you receive without clutching. This is what you must learn now. This is what you came for. There is nothing else to do today.

Extend love and receive love. Pay no attention to anything else and ask no others questions. This is your true Answer to anything that confronts you today.

126

Answering the Call

o o o o o o o o o o o o o o o o o o o o o o o o o o o o o o o o

The Call is universal. It goes on all the time everywhere . . . many hear It, but few will answer. Yet it is all a matter of time. Everyone will answer in the end, but the end can be a long, long way off . . . And each one saves a thousand years of time as the world judges it. To the Call Itself time has no meaning.

-A Course in Miracles

The problem with physical incarnation is that once you arrive you tend to be easily distracted and caught up in meaningless things. This is a deliberate attempt by the ego to tempt you to forget who you are and why you came here. It is quite effective in its own way but the Call is so strong that it requires ever-increasing effort to push it down. More shopping, more eating, more sleeping, drinking, drugging, TV watching and such to keep you asleep to your Divine Destiny.

When you are asleep to Who you really are, you will find yourself at various times in places you have no business being, doing things you have no business doing and Something inside you will say, *"This is not me!"* It is the reminder of the call and it is the opportunity for a miracle. But YOU must be willing and determined to do whatever it takes to do the right thing even while it still feels wrong. You must begin to put yourself in alignment with the people, places and situations which will remind you of you Who you are instead of who you are not. Your free will is not interfered with. You always have choice and as you begin making good choices it will become easier to continue to make them. You will be given all the Help that you need as long as you continue to show up for your Calling.

The Call is not a job. It's not even a real "doing" though you will certainly be led to do various things along the way. The Call is to teach love by demonstrating it. And it is a miraculous act of self-love to accept your part in the Great Campaign - and this begins by remembering that you are an extension of God Himself, clothed in flesh and sent into a darkened world to bear the Light - a personal Ambassador, not special, no different than anyone else except perhaps in your degree of willingness. More and more as you begin to honor your role, you will not become arrogant but supremely humble as through your own example you teach others how to answer the Call for Teachers. It begins right now if you are willing. Your part is to say, "Yes God, Here I am. Use me. I am willing. Lead me and make good use of me today."

127

Seeking God is Unnecessary

o o o o o o o o o o o o o o o o o o o o o o o o o o o o o

If you cannot hear the Voice for God, it is because you do not choose to listen.

-A Course in Miracles

There is no need to seek for God because there is no time, place or state where God is absent. But what you may need to do is fine-tune your receiver. You live in a world full of various forms of static and distractions which seem to interfere with your listening: TV, movies, internet, traffic, self-medicating, attack thoughts, worrying, cell phones, music blaring into earphones, billboards, an over-scheduled 24/7 lifestyle and all kinds of electric vibrations flowing through your airwaves. Your atmosphere is quite dense and though the God frequency can easily cut through it all, it is still a more subtle vibration and requires you to practice locking onto the signal.

It is a discipline. The God signal goes out everywhere all the time and is available to everyone. There is no way to earn it or become "worthy" of it, but there are things that you may need to do in order to improve your ability to hear. Meditation or "quieting the mind" is very helpful. The same is true of prayer, a short period of fasting combined with prayer, reading spiritual texts, long walks in nature, singing songs of praise and joyful thanksgiving, feeding the hungry, visiting the sick, doing forgiveness work, body work, giving and tithing - all the various forms of spiritual practice are not ways to invite God in because God is already present. They are not ways of pleasing or appeasing some far off entity. They are simply the ways that you learn to become a finely-tuned intuitional instrument of the Divine because they more deeply reflect your true nature. These practices open your centers and help to undo the inner-chaos and static.

You say you want peace and then you overstimulate and terrorize yourself. You say you want to feel the Divine Presence and then you fill your mind with thoughts that are not a vibrational match to the Divine Frequency. Instead, become willing to have the Holy Spirit lead you to whatever changes in you will make your more available and in tune with the more subtle vibrations. Like anything else, the more you do it, the easier it will become. It takes discipline and determination in the beginning, but once you have some momentum, it becomes a new and dynamic miracle habit. This is not about deprivation and a dour religious attitude of sacrifice. Try different practices until you find the ones that feel most helpful and joyful to you and you may find that each day you are doing something different than the day before. It is not the form that matters but rather the result. The happier and more joyful and centered you are, the more open your centers are to receiving the God vibe.

128

Ask, Believe, Receive

o o o o o o o o o o o o o o o o o o o o o o o o o o o o o o o o o

There is nothing my holiness cannot do.

-A Course in Miracles

The clearer a channel you become, the faster and more effortlessly the manifestations of good will come *through* you. There is an important distinction there that will bring your spirit a greater peace and joy, which is remembering that nothing comes to you, it comes through you. Nothing is ever for you or for anyone alone. Anything that cannot be shared is not worth having to begin with and whatever is hoarded is lost to you. You are meant to be a vessel, a conduit through which endless gifts flow forth to the world - and they are there for you to use as well. Hold onto nothing and you will always have more than enough.

The process couldn't be more simple. Your main part is that after steps 1 and 2 you must NOT interfere or rush the process along.

1. Ask - that the Divine Will be done in your life in totally harmonious and joyful ways

2. Believe - in a kind and friendly Universe which responds in perfect timing and in perfect ways

3. Receive - as graciously and joyfully as possible knowing that nothing ever really belongs to anyone but is simply a gift on-loan for as long as it would be helpful to serve the Greater Plan.

129

The Future is a Myth

o o o o o o o o o o o o o o o o o o o o o o o o o o o o o

I place the future in the hands of God.

-A Course in Miracles

Today is the future you worried about. Does it feel like the future to you? Of course not because it is simply another illusion the the ego tries to put around reality; an imaginary box. There is only the ever-present now stretching out into Eternity. The "future" is mostly another way to terrify yourself or to distract yourself from the now with fantasies.

You spend so much time wondering what is going to happen and trying to control possible future outcomes that you often ruin your experience of today. The reality is that today lived properly and consciously tends to take care of tomorrow. Stop worrying about tomorrows manna and focus on gratitude for today's daily bread. As you practice gratitude in your now more consistently you'll find that this illusory future never does arrive but your now continues to be an ever-unfolding path of joy.

To place the future in the hands of God is not irresponsible. The Divine Wisdom within you can ONLY be heard in the now. If there are things to do to prepare for the future, you will be guided and led WITHOUT FEAR. Animals don't worry about the future yet because they are always in contact with the Greater Wisdom, they instinctively know exactly what to do and when to do it. Remember again, the birds hold no committee meetings nor "brainstorming" sessions to decide when to fly south for the winter. They are all tapped into the same Infinite Source and know exactly the day, the hour, the moment to take flight. And you, little miracle worker, are certainly as precious as any bird. It's just that your worry interferes with the Signals from Source. Let it go today. Be present. Be joyful. Be grateful - and place the future in the hands of God.

130

Miracle Worker's Agreements: Read Daily for 30 Days

I take 100% responsibility for my own life, happiness, healing and what I get out of each day and every experience. I do not expect others to fix me or make me happy.

*I agree to love myself **no matter what!***

I agree to do whatever it takes to stay centered and clear.

I take responsibility for communicating my feelings appropriately.

I commit to daily spiritual renewal through conscious contact with God in whatever way works best for me.

I agree to communicate when something is not working for me.

I do not have to communicate if doing so is unsafe or would harm myself or another. I seek Divine Guidance regarding appropriateness.

I will express my love and gratitude to those around me whenever I can.

I agree to ask for help when I need it. I let go of expecting others to read my mind or know what I want and need.

I release my loved ones from my expectations that they should meet those needs and wants once I have communicated them - I will not manipulate, threaten, whine or project guilt.

I agree to communicate my feelings as best I can without attack or blame.

I will help others as best I can without taking responsibility for their lives, happiness or experiences.

I release others from participating in my self-destructive patterns.

I release myself from participating in the self-destructive patterns of others.

I agree to keep a positive mental attitude and to question my stressful thoughts rather than believing them without investigation.
I agree to learn with joy and to trust the process.

I will learn to say no without making excuses or feeling guilty.

131

Consult a Higher Authority

I am under no laws but God's.

-A Course in Miracles

When one of your most beloved and famous author's son was in a car accident which nearly killed his body, the doctor told her that her son would never walk again. She looked him right in the eyes and said, *"What do you know? I've consulted a Higher Authority!"* And of course, her son is walking because she rejected the fear that tried to enter her.

Miracle worker, part of Our job is to keep reminding you to consult the Higher Authority on a very regular basis - to become spiritually biased rather than factually correct. What is most important are not the facts of your life or the world around you. What is MOST important is your Consciousness. Your Consciousness will determine your experience far more than any facts ever could. Your Consciousness is the mix of your mental vibration, your emotional vibration and your spiritual vibration. If you lead with Spirit dominance, your Consciousness will be clear, high and miracle-ready because your thoughts and emotions will be brought into service of the Spirit rather than passively allowing them to try to lead.

Now this mother did not refuse medical treatment for her son - did not remove him from the hospital - did not take the doctor off the case.

She let him do what he knew how to do. But what she remembered is that his thoughts, opinions and observations were not the final word. He was speaking from a limited puny human statistical mindset. She was living by Consciousness rather than by facts so she allowed him to do his job and paid no attention to his predictions or probabilities.

The world reports only the facts, figures and limitations. And they are skewed towards fear in order to keep your mind limited and manipulated. The economy, the latest sicknesses, your ever-aging body, what is possible and probable for you, the environment, the current wars are all told from the most negative fear-based consciousness and usually in an attempt to sell you something that will "save"you. And when you believe these "facts" without question your consciousness begins to resonate to that frequency and you are bound by the laws of time and space and matter and man.

But YOU are under no laws but God's. You have consulted a Higher Authority. For you, the facts on the evening news are just an interesting footnote telling you what the current dominant consciousness of limitation is believing today. Have no part of it miracle worker. Stop terrifying yourself with the things that increase your disconnection from your Higher Awareness. When something terrifying or even mildly disturbing is reported to you, say to yourself clearly and calmly, *"That has nothing to do with me. I have consulted a Higher Authority and I am under no laws but God's."* Then, ask for Holy Spirit to guide you and in how to think and what, if anything, you are to do. If you are guided to take the medicine, buy the policy, or to cancel the trip - then, it is coming as direct Guidance from Source rather than as the fearful act of a limited consciousness.

132

Give It To the Staff To Handle

o o o o o o o o o o o o o o o o o o o o o o o o o o o o o o

My control can take over everything that does not matter, while my guidance can direct everything that does.

-A Course in Miracles

Remember that We told you that there is a big difference between being merely busy and being truly fruitful? We want to keep reminding you of this because being busy is often an ego strategy to keep you from inner-fellowship. The ego will keep you preoccupied with a never-ending "to-do" list so that you never seem to have time to fulfill your function, do the things that really matter, quiet your mind, spend time with Spirit or have a moment to remember Who you really are.

Starting today, We want you to make a "to-do" list for your Angel Staff as well as your own list. We want to teach you to delegate and you begin right now by dividing up your list and keeping on yours only the things that you really want to do. Remember, We invented synchronicity! So don't you think We may have a better idea than you of how to arrange all the time, resources, people and situations for things to go smoothly and so easily that things seem to be doing themselves? We know how to find the best nanny, file the report, coordinate the party, locate the most honest mechanic, align you with the best employer for you, get an appointment when they aren't taking new patients . . . oh, and collapse time and space if necessary too. Or, you can go right ahead and continue to try to do it all yourself. Free will is the name of the game here.

Now quite often We will use your hands to get a job done, but it will still be done in a timing and in a manner that is much more efficient than when you thought it was all up to YOU to do. Simply stay in tune with those little inner-nudges of inspiration and follow them faithfully whether they are making phone calls, asking for help or simply paying much more attention to the answers We are sending all the time that you often turn down or ignore. Remember, you have to be PRESENT to win. In particular you can put on that list each week those things that you really don't WANT to do - the things that you have been avoiding and putting on your own list week after week and sometimes even month after month. Put it on Our list and then just be willing to see what happens.

It's why it's called a Course in MIRACLES, remember?

133

Change The Station

o o o o o o o o o o o o o o o o o o o o o o o o o o o o o o o o o

You may still complain about fear, but you nevertheless persist in making yourself fearful. I have already indicated that you cannot ask me to release you from fear, I know that it does not exist, but you do not. If I intervened between your thoughts and their results, I would be tampering with a basic law of cause and effect; the most fundamental law there is. I would hardly help you if I depreciated the power of your own thinking. This would be in direct opposition to the purpose of this course. It is much more helpful to remind you that you do not guard your thoughts carefully enough.

-A Course in Miracles

It's impossible to listen to two radio stations at the same time and yet humans sometimes try to tune into two very different stations at the same time and wonder why all they hear is static. You cannot hear Radio KGOD and radio KFUK at the same time. They are two extremely different frequencies. So, you either go back and forth between them or you aren't locked onto either one and all you hear is crackling static and buzzing.

Don't expect to hear the Voice for God when you are frantic or freaking out or even in deep despair or grief. You are not in the proper vibrational receiving mode. This is where your daily discipline really pays off. If you've been quieting your mind on a daily basis all along, even when things were going very well, then you have some mental musculature to do it when things seem to get rough. This allows you to quiet yourself enough to become a matching receiver to radio KGOD so you can lock onto the signal and receive the peace and comfort that you deserve.

But again, the responsibility lies with YOU, always and forever. You cannot turn on your TV and watch channel 4 and then complain that they are not broadcasting the channel 27 shows to you. YOU are responsible for the station you tune into and if you only think to tune into KGOD when you are in crisis, then you won't have the necessary inner-discipline to stay locked onto the signal when things are not to your liking.

That's why it's called spiritual PRACTICE. There is Principle and there is Practice. Humans tend to prefer the principle because it is the visioning and inspirational part. But it is the actual PRACTICE that will change your experience of life. What station are you listening to today?

134

No One Has Been Assigned to You

o o o o o o o o o o o o o o o o o o o o o o o o o o o o o o o o

My happiness and my function are one.

-A Course in Miracles

It is YOUR job to make you happy. No one has been assigned to you. No one is coming - not ever. It is 100% your responsibility to make yourself happy. Your spouse is not going to do it. Your children can't do it. The government, church, society, economy, your career, your body, shopping, drugs, fame, wealth, nature . . . none of them are going to make you happy. The ball is totally in your court every single day all day long.

Today and every day your job is to make yourself happy by CHOOSING to be happy. It is about the thoughts your think and the way that you perceive and focus on life. Many of you deny yourself happiness and then pout that the world is not bending over backwards to make you happy. The fact is, the Universe merely mirrors back to you your own thoughts and perceptions. If you are busy making yourself happy, your world will reflect that back to you. If you are denying yourself happiness, waiting for someone or something to do it for you, your world will reflect a waiting withhold mentality towards you too. It's all just a big mirror.

And by the same token, you cannot make anyone else happy either. You cannot make your boss, spouse, friends, family or society happy. You can do what they want and temporarily please their egos, but you cannot actually give them a sense of true happiness that lasts for more than a very short time. Everyone has been assigned THEMSELVES.

And what you find is that this is not selfish at all. If you make yourself happy every day, you are a much more pleasant energy to be around and you are a Light unto the world through your example - and notice too that when you are truly happy you are much kinder, more generous, compassionate and forgiving to all those around you. This is the gift of choosing your own happiness.

135

Focus, Focus, Focus

o o o o o o o o o o o o o o o o o o o o o o o o o o o o o

Perception has a focus. It is this that gives consistency to what you see. Change but this focus, and what you behold will change accordingly . . . remove your focus on your brother's sins, and you experience the peace that comes from faith in sinlessness.

-A Course in Miracles

We are so thrilled with the progress you are making miracle worker. You are really learning how to shift your energies and focus so much more efficiently. Remember that we are going for penguin step progress here, not perfection. Please don't forget to celebrate every step forward!

And We want to remind you again that it is much much more helpful to Us in arranging your life if you will keep telling Us what you appreciate rather than what you didn't like about past and present situations. It is so easy to focus on the negative in people and situations when you are talking with those close to you - do not give into this temptation to focus on the errors.

For example, you may have had several relationships over the past few years that did not "work out" the way that you wanted them to and you sometimes have a tendency to put your attention on the aspects of the person or situation that was not to your liking. THIS IS A HUGE FUCKING MISTAKE! BIG, BIG, BIG MISTAKE! We don't care

243

what you don't want and don't like. To focus on what you don't want and don't like is like getting into your car and programming into your GPS the exact location of where you don't want to go.

What is far more helpful to Us is for you to keep a master list of everything that you DID like about that person or situation or about yourself and any positives it brought out in you. GIVE 100% OF YOUR ATTENTION AND FOCUS TO WHAT WORKED! This becomes your dominant consciousness and is what give the laws of cause and effect their orders for what you are interested in.

This works with jobs, relationships, homes, money, health and everything else. If you had a few dates this year - tell Us ONLY the positive aspects that you appreciate about the person or situation that you would like to see in your future. Do the same thing with anything in your life where you would like to see expansion and growth. Whatever you focus on increases - but you already knew that. We're just reminding you because you are doing so well that we see greater and greater things for you as you fine-tune your laser-like focus in the days to come.

136

Be a JOYFUL Giver

o o o o o o o o o o o o o o o o o o o o o o o o o o o o o o o o

To give and to receive are one in Truth.

-A Course in Miracles

The Universe is nothing but Consciousness and that Consciousness is made up of vibration - pulsating energy. EVERYTHING is vibrational and energetic and everything you do is infused with the energy that was within you when you did it. These are your creations and they reflect your energy.

Too many spiritual folks give with fear or from a sense of duty or sacrifice or to get something back and then wonder why the tithing laws don't totally open the windows of Heaven and pour our their blessings. Look at it this way, when a loved one does something for you out of fear, duty or sacrifice, or to get something back from you - what is the energy that gets communicated to you and does it feel like the windows of Heaven opening up in your relationship? Probably not.

To people who understand and apply the laws of the Universe there is a tremendous rush that comes from giving. They cannot wait to give back out a portion of all that they receive and it's done so automatically and quickly that it's like the rhythm of breathing in and breathing out.

Give happily, joyfully, and with the inner-reverence and awareness that you are planting seeds in God's garden to help it grow. When you give to the person, place or institution from which you receive your spiritual food, you are planting a blessing so that it will serve others well and you are also planting something that YOU will harvest as well. Don't just give unconsciously or from a fearful consciousness. Take time to bless your offering with joy and abundance and gratitude to Source. This is a shift that can make a huge difference in your own experience of a greater opening and willingness not only to give but to receive as well.

137

The Only Thing That's Really True

o o o o o o o o o o o o o o o o o o o o o o o o o o o o o o

Truth will correct all errors in my mind.

-A Course in Miracles

The only thing that's really true right now . . . is person sitting reading. Everything else is just some story existing in mind. And the question is whether it is a story that you are using to terrify, disturb, motivate or upset yourself or someone else with or whether it is a happy joyful story of love and peace. If the story is a happy one - it is part of the Happy Dream and you can simply drink in the vision.

If it is not, then it's best to question the thoughts you are believing and come back to the awareness of the only thing that's really true right now. Stories are not facts. They are interpretations of facts woven into a tale of sorrow or of joy.

For instance, cancer is just a word to describe cellular activity in the body. There's nothing scary about that. But you have a whole world that has made that word part of a very scary STORY which means this and means that. Unquestioned, this word can be woven into a story so terrifying that you can barely breathe. But, if you tell your dog she has cancer, no problem. She just goes on living in her now and when she feels good she runs and plays and doesn't even think about her cells. However, a human who believes his story will often ruin even the days when he feels great by terrifying himself with a story of cellular activity that is having no effect on his energy that day.

The same is true with money, jobs, relationships, sex, the economy, family, your future or the past. Facts are rarely the problem. It is the interpretation and story we tell about facts that are usually the blockage to your miracle.

It's all about the story. If you are loving your story today and it feels good - go for it baby. But if your story is disturbing you, whether it is about you or someone else, you can either question the story and drop it, or you can tell a better version. It's up to you miracle worker and that is very very good news.

138

The Love Impulse

○ ○

. . . everything that comes from love is a miracle.

-A Course in Miracles

Love is the impulse of life and the law propels that impulse into manifestation. Too many metaphysicians make far too much of the law of attraction, forgetting that it is merely the servant of the Love Impulse. When you put the law first, then fearful scarcity egoic thinking may be the creative force. Love must come before the law. The feminine energy must guide the masculine force. The Mother-Father God loved and THEN created life from that love. Put first things first.

Today is a day to look and see, what is the love impulse within you guiding you towards? The most profound law of attraction is NOT what you are attracting, but what is attracting YOU?

139

Don't Be Discouraged

○ ○

Only infinite patience produces immediate results.

-A Course in Miracles

Miracle worker, the path that you are on is really very simple, but it is not an easy one. It is not easy because the ego will sometimes attack you with such viciousness that if you are not standing firmly in your truth it can take you to the ground in an instant.

Much of the progress that you have made and are making is invisible to eyes that judge according to appearances. As you focus on the externals it may seem like the world is rushing ahead of you while you are standing still or even seemingly moving backwards. This is exactly the kind of attack the ego can be expected to make when you are making the most real progress.

THIS IS THE TIME TO STAND FIRM in your resolve. Do not become weary in well-doing. Continue to choose the highest thoughts available to you at any given moment and practice using the power of your words to encourage, soothe and uplift yourself. Do not give into temptation. The harvest is so close now miracle worker, but be aware that it will take perhaps more energy to reap than you have expended already! Bringing in the Harvest is an exciting time but it will call on all your reserves so don't be SO anxious to begin that process. You are in that quiet time between the sowing and reaping. Don't get antsy and start digging up the seeds to see if they've taken root or you will simply ruin the crop! Yet, even if you do, there is another one coming behind that one - and another and another. The seasons continue to cycle all the time and while in one area of your life it may be winter, in some other area it is yet another spring beginning.

Walk in faith during this quiet time. Hone your inner-instruments so that you can sense what is happening when "nothing is happening." If you can stay "on course" through the in-between time, you will in proper time gather a harvest that will nourish you and generations yet to come. This is not mere hyperbole or self-glorification because you know by now that We don't deal with you in that way. Remember, you are not simply living a life, you are on a teaching mission and We have need of **joyful** teachers. So please spend this in-between time making yourself happy. Do the things you love no matter how simple. Get proper rest. Read, walk, visit with uplifting friends, be careful what you put into your body - the harvest time will be quite busy and We want you to be in excellent condition and ready to let the Great Rays shine through you. Practice patience, diligence, compassion and spend some time each day actively encouraging yourself. Remember that contrary to your world of illusions, in Our world slow is fast, and fast is slow.

140

Program the GPS

○ ○

The one true and holy thing that you can say about the past is that it is not here.

-A Course in Miracles

Remember, it doesn't matter where you ***don't*** want to go today. It doesn't matter how lost you are or how far off track you seem to be. It doesn't matter how you got so messed up or whose fault it was. The Universal GPS system is simply waiting for you to program into it WHERE YOU WANT TO GO NOW.

All this means is that the Universe is ready to start over again every single moment. It's only YOU who thinks that it's going to take x amount of time to get over this or that. The Holy Spirit's GPS system doesn't care what the economy is like, how old you are, how out of shape you are, how long it's been since your last romance, what country or town you live in, your family history or genetics, your bankruptcy and low credit score, what your parents did or didn't do to/for you, what the prognosis is, your neurotic self-sabotaging patterns or that some "therapist" says that it takes 2 years to recover from whatever you just went through.

All it wants to know is, where next? How do you WANT to feel today? What are the thoughts you want to cultivate? What energy do you want to stimulate and call forth?

So, you can sit here trying to explain and justify how you got so lost and tell some myth about how time and the past has something to do with what is possible for you now- or you can program your destination and get right back on the road again. It's always your choice.

141

The Heart is Not Safe

o o o o o o o o o o o o o o o o o o o o o o o o o o o o o o o
In my defenselessness, my safety lies.

-A Course in Miracles

Love is not safe. Relationships are not safe. It is not safe to give your heart to anyone or to anything. But, you didn't come here to be safe. You came here to live and to love. You cannot live and love and protect your heart at the same time.

If you truly love animals and fill your life with pets, you will have to watch them grow old, get sick and die. If you have children, you will have to watch them be hurt by others, fail at some things, and perhaps they will get sick and die before you do too.

People leave, break promises, fall short of your expectations of them, lie, cheat and are often weak. And even if they behave perfectly, it may hurt you that they go off to work without you each day. Friends sometimes move far away. Life cannot be controlled. The ego is very easily disappointed and disturbed by change. The problem is not that people are so full of character defects nor that life is so unpredictable. The problem is that you think they shouldn't be. The problem is that so many humans think they can protect their hearts and still love. But this is impossible.

Love is about taking down the fences from around your heart knowing that not only is it possible that you may be hurt - it's a guarantee. This tiny little protected "self" is definitely going to be hurt - no matter what. Even if you pull back and put yourself on the bench - still, there will be a long dull ache from withholding from what you came here to do.

Love is the greatest sport in the world and like most sports, you're gonna get dirty and have some injuries. But what fun to get off the bench and get into the game!! Remember, you didn't come here to be an observer. You didn't come here to be in the audience watching from the stands. You came here to play. The only thing that's different is that in this game there is no competition, no winners, no losers. This sport is about exercising the heart - the love muscle.

So, sometimes you may need a little time out to sit on the bench and get your knees wrapped and have a few sips of water and catch your breath. That's cool. But, don't sit too long. Don't let yourself get stiff and cranky. Get back out there and feel the thrilling rush of playing. The little self is never safe, but the real you can never be hurt.

142

Find Things to Be Happy About

○ ○

The first obstacle that peace must flow across is your desire to get rid of it.

-A Course in Miracles

We know how you often declare that you want peace and happiness in your life and that you do NOT want drama and upset anymore. This is certainly true on the conscious level of your awareness once you've gotten some learning under your belt. But what you may not be quite so aware of is the unconscious urge towards the very upset and drama that you say you don't want. If this were not so, the phrase "self-sabotage" would not be such a popular one.

In this case We are not even talking about the outer drama of circumstances at all. We are talking about the ways in which you sometimes have a tendency to create drama in your thoughts at times when you could just as easily be feeling peaceful and full of joy. This is because some of you have a tendency to become uncomfortable when things are flowing easily and going well.

You may have some uninterrupted time driving in the car when your thoughts could turn towards the lovely scenery, how blessed you are, the wonderful people in your life, the opportunities you've been given -but instead your mind begins to drift to thoughts like, *"Hmm,*

let me do an inventory to see who isn't doing things my way, what isn't
working perfectly yet, what I have not yet achieved or isn't being given to
me, what went wrong yesterday and last week, and how the world isn't
really pleasing me." Of course, it's not that overt but it boils down
to that at times. The ego mind always goes toward the negative in an
attempt to push the presence of peace away. But remember, it is YOUR
job to make you happy and you do this by your determination to find
things to focus on that stimulate happiness.

You COULD think about what a lovely dinner date you had with
that really wonderful person last week and what a great time you both
had. But ego decides to focus on the fact that you never heard from
that person again. In reality does that make the time you spent together
less enjoyable? NO!! But you are free to push away the peace and joy
in your present by focusing on whatever details will make peace most
unwelcome.

Peace, joy and happiness ARE already at home in you. It is up to
YOU whether you will make them welcome today or push them out in
an attempt to make them homeless. Look around miracle worker and
become a detective who is endlessly looking for the clues and evidence
that prove you have every reason to be happy today.

143

Be Conscious of What You Activate in Them

○ ○

In everyone you see but the reflection of what you choose to have him be to you.

-A Course in Miracles

Reflect for a moment on the vibrational nature of the Universe. As a part of the Universe, YOU are vibrational in nature, forever in motion on every level. And like a tuning fork, the vibrational tone that you strike awakens that same vibrational tone in those around you who have made themselves available for that note.

Therefore, you would do well to be careful what you activate in those around you because once it IS active, YOU will have to deal with it. And you would do well to activate that which you WANT to call forth in others.

Many of you bring up subjects and things that are greatly upsetting to you and this awakens that same vibration in the people around you so that now you are increasing the vibration of the very thing that disturbs and upsets you. And while you are responsible for you own vibration and have tremendous influence and control over it - you cannot control others so once you've awakened that vibration in them, you cannot control it.

This is a matter of focus and attention. You may need to cultivate the habit of thinking before you speak to consider what vibrational tone you want to activate in the relationship in front of you. Your complaining will activate the dissatisfaction in those around you. Your gratitude will activate the gratitude in those around you. And if the person you are with does not want that particular vibration activated within them - your energies will not match up and at least for the time being, you will tend to drift apart until your energies match up again.

So just slow down a little bit and consider *"What are the dominant energies I want to activate within myself and others now?"* Then, focus on that and keep striking that chord within you and soon enough you will find that everything around you begins to shift and move in order to harmonize with that same vibration!

144

Your Elimination List

o o o o o o o o o o o o o o o o o o o o o o o o o o o o o o o o o o o o

I can be free of suffering today.

-A Course in Miracles

There is nothing proactive about murmuring and complaining. It only keeps in your consciousness those things that you do not want. And while anything is active in your consciousness it is a magnetic point of attraction and you will continue to experience the very things you say you don't want.

If you want to take a positive action, We suggest you make an "elimination list" and write down everything that no longer serves you in living the life you want to live. This is not a "getting rid of" nor is it a strategy - you are merely releasing to the Universe all that is on this list in order to have it be lifted from you willingly and with great ease.

Your elimination list will be comprised of thoughts, patterns and beliefs that no longer serve you but it will also include certain kinds of unhealthy relationships, physical conditions, indebtedness, habits, addictions, old behaviors - anything that it is time to let go of.

At the bottom of the list, write a prayer treatment releasing it all to Spirit to be lifted from you in ONLY the most harmonious and IDEAL ways and timing. After your elimination list, it is time to work on your YES list, which is the next entry in this book.

145

Your YES List

o o o o o o o o o o o o o o o o o o o o o o o o o o o o o o o o o o

Now let a new perception come to me.

-A Course in Miracles

After you've made an elimination list, your mind is free to think NEW thoughts. This is the opportunity for you to begin to expand your consciousness to envision the life that you want. It's not a "shopping list" experience where you are just mindlessly filling a list with all the things you think you want. Do not make of this an ego exercise in greed.

No, this is a FEELING list. Whatever you write on this list must awaken the Divine YES!! within you as you write it. Make this an on-going list which you are adapting and changing as you become clearer and clearer on what it is that your deepest Self is really opening up to channel into your life.

You can look at your elimination list and let this be part of the catalyst of clarity. If you are releasing one-sided relationships in which you are always "saving" people, what do you choose to channel into your life instead? Be specific and yet relaxed. This should stimulate only GOOD pleasant feelings. If it becomes stressful or you start strategizing on how to MAKE IT happen, put it away because your ego has taken over again. Then you can work on it again when you are centered in your Christ-Self again.

Imagine the kinds of feelings you want to have, the words you want to speak and hear spoken to you, the kinds of experiences you are choosing to be a part of now. Make it playful, fun and inspiring for YOU. This is not a list of "shoulds" about your life - it is a place to dream, vision and tap into the Universal creative magnetic Force that holds galaxies in place.

146

Expand Your Container

o o o o o o o o o o o o o o o o o o o o o o o o o o o o o o

*You cannot spend five minutes in the morning affirming that all is
well and then spend the rest of the day proving that it is not.*

-Ernest Holmes

Two of the most common reasons that people live in less than the
plenty that is God's will for them is that they are either holding onto
their own good without generously giving and sharing it fearlessly or
they are not fully open to receiving.

Miracle worker, We want to encourage you today to begin to
expand your consciousness of receptivity. There is always work to be
done in expanding your capacity to allow in even more good. You are
a channel and a vessel for God's Light to pour through in all its forms
and formlessness and if your valve is not open, or is only slightly open,
you are blocking that good from coming through even though you
may SAY that you want more good and are even actively praying for
it all the time. The fact is that many of you pray and then actively
work AGAINST your own prayers through self-sabotaging behaviors,
or through words of doubt and negativity. Do not pray faith and then
speak fear. It is like writing with one hand and erasing with the other.

You cannot pray your way out of problems that you continue to
behave your way into. YOU must change in order to receive all the

blessings that God has for you. We would love for you to spend the next week or so in contemplation with the Holy Spirit allowing It to reveal to you the ways that you may not be fully open to receiving AND the ways that you may be working against your own prayers.

One way to expand your container is with gratitude and appreciation. Learn to be a grateful and gracious receiver. Learn to say YES to your good when it comes along and learn to say NO to the things that no longer serve your new expanded consciousness!

147

God IS Love

o o o o o o o o o o o o o o o o o o o o o o o o o o o o o

Fear of the will of God is one of the strangest beliefs the human mind has ever made.

-A Course in Miracles

You cannot both love and fear God. Love casts out fear and fear casts out the awareness of love's presence. They simply cannot co-exist. If you fear God or God's will then you can be sure that you have a man-made mythical insane and unstable egoic God who needs to be fired.

The Great Mother-Father Presence is sane, stable and knows nothing but love, love and more love. What's to be afraid of?

How much love can you handle today? And if you are afraid, what stressful thoughts are you believing?

148

Make a Decision

○ ○

The power of decision is my own.

-A Course in Miracles

One of the most powerful phrases in all of the Universe are the words *"I've decided."* This is not the arrogance of the ego, but the certainty of Spirit within you.

Miracle worker, when the real You calmly and serenely states as a fact, *"I've decided,"* there is no resistance nor doubt in it whatsoever. You are not going to force or "make" anything happen. You simply state a fact that you have come to accept as true.

In fact, thousands of times a day *"I've decided"* is implied as you go about your day. You've decided to pick up the mail, to make a phone call, to make a sandwich, to change the TV channel - all without fanfare or doubt. All of life is like this except in the story you tell yourself. When you think you need to *make* something happen, you have not truly decided. You've made up a story about how you have to use your self-will against an unwilling world or situation. But you know from past experience that when you are clear, when you have confidently decided without neediness or desperation but from an inner desire of the soul, things tend to move rather quickly and without unnecessary strain. There is work to do, but it is working with not against. Most any calm clear decision you make *that does not interfere with the free-will of another* will start the Universe moving toward its fulfillment almost immediately.

Start to practice this more - in private. Do not speak it in front of others for a while for they may project their own fears and strategies onto you before you are strong enough to handle it. When you are alone, get used to calmly stating out loud, *"I've decided . . . "* even about the most mundane of things. Then notice the difference between when you feel calm and confident within and when you get a sense of doubt or start strategizing or needing to force something to happen. Do this frequently for a while so that you become more and more aware of the different energies within you as you begin to play with the Power that is within you. *"I've decided to heal. I've decided to become happily married. I've decided to live my life honestly and openly. I've decided I will run my own business successfully and with great fun. I've decided I deserve to be happy. I've decided to stop doing things I don't want to do. I've decided to become a wonderful parent. I've decided to get clean and sober. I've decided to go back to school. "* Your whole world begins to move when you make a real decision and you don't have to know HOW it will happen. Your job is a clear calm what, the Universe will guide and reveal the how. And the more light-hearted you are when you make your statement, the more effortlessly and quickly it will tend to occur.

Wishy-washy decisions bring about wishy-washy manifestations. Did you ever hear of a wishy-washy miracle worker? Make a clear calm confident decision, surrender it to Spirit and move forward. You will receive Guidance, correction, signs, resources and all that you need to see it through so long as you stay in non-attachment and non-resistance. At this level, it is not you "doing" anymore. You are the midwife to the miracle.

149

Prepare YOURSELF and the Opportunity Will Come

o o o o o o o o o o o o o o o o o o o o o o o o o o o o o o o

My brother, choose once again.

-A Course in Miracles

Once you've made a clear decision about something, Life will begin to rise up to meet you as you continue to show up and practice being present. This is very important - being present and available is not possible if you are nervous, attached to outcomes, needy, and have a specific agenda beyond letting the Divine Plan unfold.

Some of you tend to waste a lot of time trying to manufacture opportunities when if you simply focused your energies on stimulating the joy within yourselves, We would be able to bring to you the best opportunities without your interference. We know you think you are helping Us, but you're not. You're getting in the way. Work on YOU so that you'll be happy and ready for the opportunities as We send them your way.

150

You Can Also Change Your Mind

○ ○

No one who reaches this far can make the wrong decision, although he can delay. And there is no part of the journey that seems more hopeless and futile than standing where the road branches, and not deciding on which way to go.

-A Course in Miracles

To the devoted miracle worker, decisions and commitments are not made willy-nilly or without deeply seeking Guidance and Help from Heaven. But too many miracle workers stand in paralysis at times, afraid to make a strong choice and commit to it for fear of making a mistake.

But sweet one, if you have truly sought Direction, then even going off in the wrong direction will still lead you home because you are not alone. As you remain in contact with Source and your Inner-Guidance you will feel within whether it is appropriate to change your mind and go another way.

In fact, there have been times when it was quite helpful for you to explore the "wrong" direction with a full commitment because that is how you discovered that it was not the right choice for you. Standing at the branching of the road not making a choice simply delayed learning.

In other words, you may have dreamed of starting your own business for years but were too vague and wishy-washy about it to ever move forward. Then, finally you got sick of talking about it and opened your business and ran it for a year, in the process discovering that you hated every minute of it.

This was not a failure at all - it is part of the process of clarity. The successful miracle worker does not allow pride to prevent learning even if that means falling down in public. Only those who've sat down at the branching of their own road will judge you. Those who are fully-engaged in their own journey will simply smile at you as they recognize another student-teacher on the road.

151

People WILL Push Your Buttons – Let Em

○ ○

Do you prefer that you be right or happy?

-A Course in Miracles

Of course you've noticed quite a while ago that the thing about people is that a lot of them are "a pain in the ass." This is the ego's evaluation of anyone who pushes your buttons. And the ego's answer to this is to get rid of those people who are always going around pushing your buttons - unless they are a close loved one and then the ego decides to go on an all-out campaign to reform the person to get them to stop pushing your buttons.

The one thing that is rarely if ever considered is, *"What the fuck am I doing with all these buttons anyhow? Maybe it's ME that is the problem with all these damn buttons! Why am I so easily upset, disturbed and offended?"*

Healing is disconnecting your own buttons rather than trying to control your environment so that they never get pushed. A miracle worker is one who is nearly impossible to offend and who is not living in reactiveness to outside stimulus. This is the level where We desire to work with you most. As you begin to question your own stressful thoughts, beliefs and concepts more - particularly the ones about how people should and shouldn't be, you will find that the things that used to put you in an uproar become less and less and less disturbing to you.

And the real miracle is that you will start to realize that those who you once thought were such a pain in the ass are now seen with kindness, warmth, compassion and a lot of good humor. So, the next time someone pushes one or several of your buttons, stop a minute and ask yourself, "*What am I doing with this ridiculous button when it isn't doing me any good at all and only makes me miserable? What thoughts am I currently believing that have me so plugged in - and would I rather be right or happy?*

152

No One Wants Your Good Advice

o o o o o o o o o o o o o o o o o o o o o o o o o o o o o o o o

Be not afraid of love. For it alone can heal all sorrow, wipe away all tears, and gently waken from his dream of pain the Son whom God acknowledges as His.

-A Course in Miracles

Miracle worker, it is time to deepen your love walk again. So many times when someone is asking you for the Love that heals, you give them advice instead. It's more comfortable for you because it keeps you in your head instead of in the Spirit.

When someone is calling out for Light or Prayer, you often give them the "good information" that you've gathered from the world of appearances. You use your ego's littleness and arrogance instead of the grandeur that God placed in you.

Every once in a great while someone will directly ask you for advice, even when what they really want is loving assurance. One of our most advanced teachers has a rule of thumb that she must be asked by the person 3 times before she will give out advice to anyone.

When someone calls out for healing, what they are calling for is nothing less than Love itself. Do not give into the temptation to advise. Give them words of LOVE, rather then telling them what to do or what to think. Remember Our Course does not say that "advice is the medium of miracles" - PRAYER is the medium of miracles. And you may want to look deeper to see how little faith you really have in prayer if you do not see it as the most powerful Force in the Universe.

"Prayer is not an old woman's idle amusement. Properly understood and applied, it is the most potent instrument of action."

-Mahatma Gandhi

153

Honor That Greed

○ ○

The Holy Spirit knows no one is special. Yet He also perceives that you have made special relationships, which He would purify and not let you destroy. However unholy the reason you made them may be, He can translate them into holiness by removing as much fear as you will let Him. You can place any relationship under His care and be sure that it will not result in pain, ***if you offer Him your willingness to have it serve no need but His.*** *All the guilt in it arises from your use of it. All the love from His. Do not, then, be afraid to let go your imagined needs, which would destroy the relationship. Your only need is His.*

-A Course in Miracles

ALL relationships start out as egoic special relationships, no exception in this world even among the best of you. Even if it is based on a higher kind of selfishness, it is still based on the thought that you could "get" something out of it, for even a feeling of altruism is somewhat selfishly based.

No worries at all. You are not expected to be pure before you come to the altar - the altar is the vessel of purification! For many people in modern metaphysics, it was greed that got them interested in the principles of manifestation. So what? Honor the greed that got you here and then release it to Spirit so that you can be purified and set free. Honor the horniness, the desire for fame and to be special, honor the fear, honor the laziness, honor the desire to be loved and taken care of, honor the "need" to be noticed and to be special, even honor the greedy desire for special spiritual states of being like samadhi, honor it all - it got you interested enough to show up. NOW, give it all to the Holy Spirit and you will be released from the suffering that it brought you. Not once and for all, but on a daily moment-by-moment basis. Prayer, quieting of the mind, deliberately seeking Guidance, reading spiritual texts and offering acts of kindness to others are the best daily spiritual practices you can cultivate.

This is NOT the "greed is good" speech because greed will kill you if you let it continue to grow within you. And if you do not have a daily spiritual practice, all these motivations and desires will keep you in a living hell that will drive you deeper and deeper into suffering as you ride the roller-coaster of hope and hopelessness, motivation and paralysis, desire and despair.

So don't worry that you are still often driven by lower needs and desires even after all your study and working on yourself. Your part is merely your willingness to show up every day in honesty - to DO your spiritual practice and to surrender all your goals, hidden agendas and strategies over and over and over again. You are never judged - you are only set back on the path lighter and freer and happier than before.

154

Directing Imagination

o o o o o o o o o o o o o o o o o o o o o o o o o o o o o o o o

You think that without the ego all would be chaos, but I assure you that without the ego all would be love.

-A Course in Miracles

Spirit speaks to you through the imagination faculty. The problem is that humans tend to think that imagination means "not real" and We are here to tell you that what you call "the imagination" merely means the faculty of mind that recognizes what is still invisible to the physical eye but which exists in the realm of pure potentiality.

In your world children are encouraged to imagine up to a certain age and then all positive imagination is deeply discouraged once humans reach school age. Whereas negative fear-based imagination is seen as helpful and even intelligent. No wonder your world is so mixed up and full of misery. You see, the ego speaks to you through the same imagination faculty, except that since the ego dominates the thought system here, it is more easily believed even though it is the father of all lies.

If you say, *"I am traveling so much I could die in a plane crash this year,"* people will try to comfort you but will also think that you are being realistic and reasonable. If you say, *"I buy so many lottery tickets I will probably win the lottery this year,"* you are laughed and ridiculed for being a dreamer who lives in a fantasy world.

EVERYONE lives in imagination MUCH of the time. WORRY is simply using the power of imagination to create something that frightens you. If you do this excessively the world will give you a label and try to medicate you out of the effects of it. But if you just worry enough each day to keep you motivated to continue doing the things that your society wants you to do, you will be somewhat rewarded and applauded for being so intelligent and reasonable. It is not reasonable - it is insanity.

We are encouraging you to imagine the things that bring you peace, joy, contentment, optimism and stimulate a courageous spirit within you. Everyone has an active vital imagination. The only question is how are you using it today?

155

Keep It Simple and Enjoy the Process

o o o o o o o o o o o o o o o o o o o o o o o o o o o o o o o o o o o

Complexity is of the ego, and is nothing more than the ego's attempt to obscure the obvious.

-A Course in Miracles

Life can be a joyful and happy adventure. But you often complicate it unnecessarily.

Your greatest asset in learning is AWARENESS, but awareness without judgment. Do not get so caught up in behavior modifications right away - let the behavior follow the new realizations in their own time if possible. Begin by gentle awareness as a kind observer rather than as an accusing prosecutor.

Watch to see when you are complicating situations with the "something extra" that you add. The "something extra" is the story you tell about whatever appears in mind.

Simplicity is not about doing less necessarily, but it is about less inner-narration as you go about the doing. For instance, you may have a very full schedule on a given day - the something extra is the story you tell yourself about it all - *"I shouldn't have to. Why is it always me?*

It's too much for one person! No one appreciates me anyhow. This is going to be a very difficult day. I better prepare for the worst. I'll never get it all done and I should get it all done. Why do I always wait til the last minute? I'm the worst mother/boss/teacher/son/partner in the world!" All of this is the complication, the something extra that is not necessary.

So just begin to notice when you are doing this. Do not make of it another enemy or use it as an excuse to judge your excellent mind. Begin by realizing that the something extra is keeping you from enjoying the process of life. Stop, take a deep breath, come back to your center and once again release the something extra as you return to simplicity. What We are teaching you is "doing" but with an attitude of non-attachment.

As you practice noticing without judgment more frequently, the stories will begin to unravel themselves. They will not hold up under the Light of awareness and you will begin to withdraw your faith in them. You CAN be extremely busy and still retain a consciousness of serene simplicity. It's all about the story you tell yourself.

156

What Do You Deserve?

o o o o o o o o o o o o o o o o o o o o o o o o o o o o o

*You don't live the life you deserve, you live the life you **think** you deserve.*

-Brother Jacob

It's important that We remind you from time to time that the Universe operates as an immense reflecting pool. All you ever see is yourself, yourself, yourself. And the Universe mirrors back to you whatever you are up to.

If you are stingy and withholding with yourself, it will look to you as if everyone around you is stingy and withholding toward you. It is the mirror effect. NO ONE can give to you what you are unwilling to give yourself.

Millions of wonderful lovely people live in utter deprivation because they have not realized what they truly deserve and they are HOPING that someone or something outside of them will one day notice them and give them what they feel they lack. It will never happen. It never has happened.

Until an inner-shift occurs within a being and they realize Who they are and are willing to claim all the gifts of the Kingdom, nothing much really changes except on a cosmetic surface level.

What do you deserve? What are you settling for? Impoverished disheartened miracle workers are not very useful to the Great Plan. Step up to the plate little miracle worker. Step into your grandeur today - one step at a time.

157

Everyone is a Channel

o o o o o o o o o o o o o o o o o o o o o o o o o o o o o o o

A sense of separation from God is the only lack you really need correct.

-A Course in Miracles

Everyone has equal access to God. There are no special people, though each student-teacher has certain gifts they excel in utilizing. You need no human to tell you God's will for you. You need no outside source to connect you to Universal Love and Intelligence.

A feeling of separation is just that, a feeling - it is not a truth at all. It is impossible that you ever be separate from your Source but you may lose your recognition of that connection. Imagine if a fish had a human mind. It might think that the ocean is a myth because it cannot SEE it or even feel it. How can you see what is all around you, in you, through you so thoroughly that there is no place where it is not - when it is clear? A fish might go to a gypsy fortune teller to connect to this invisibly possibly mythical ocean. We are trying to make a point here miracle worker.

You already are a channel for the Divine Light. It's happening whether you accept it or not. However, if you are unconscious you may very well be a somewhat constricted channel floundering around seeking what is already everywhere present.

Let yourself float more. Relax more. Trust more. FEELING the oneness is just sensory sensation. It is really not that important. All you really need to do is relax and begin to observe the evidence all around you of that infinite connection. Feelings come and go, rise and fall. They cannot be counted on because they are affected by so many things. Trust instead in the evidence that this Universal Source is always responding to your current consciousness. And as you continue to file away the overwhelming evidence each day you will not even need faith anymore because you will have replaced it with KNOWLEDGE. Even intuition is not a "feeling" - it is an inner KNOWING. Learn to trust that gut KNOWING more than your limited human senses and let your senses be the servant of Spirit rather than the guide.

158

Follow the Joy

o o o o o o o o o o o o o o o o o o o o o o o o o o o o o o o

The ego is afraid of the spirit's joy, because once you have experienced it you will withdraw all protection from the ego, and become totally without investment in fear.

-A Course in Miracles

You waste so much time trying to figure things out. You think that if you figure it all out, only then will all be well. And so you waste your creative energy living in your head, focused on the problems, problems, problems. In the end, all you are doing is becoming an expert at problems, rather than an expert on solutions and answers.

Exit the realm of the problem entirely if you want a real Answer. Go for the joy and become an expert on joy rather than an expert on your various "problems." Or if you are a really big player, you could take a lesson from one of the "fictional" characters on late night television - you could be come a "licensed joyologist."

You tend to take yourselves very seriously just when you would do well to take yourself lightly. The Truth is, the more serious seeming the problem, the greater the need to cultivate JOY because joy is the most powerful magnet in the Universe. Joy begets joy begets joy begets joy. So We suggest that you begin to follow the trail of joy thoughts rather than the trail of stressful concepts and beliefs.

What stimulates joy within you? Make a list as long as you possibly can of all that stimulates joy in you and then put it somewhere that you will see if often. Then give this more of your mental time and space than your efforts to figure out your problems. While you are focused on experiencing joy, We will have the opportunity to undo your so-called problems.

159

Attraction, Not Promotion

o o o o o o o o o o o o o o o o o o o o o o o o o o o o o o o o o

*But ask yourself if it is possible that God would have a plan for
your salvation that does not work. Once you accept His plan as
the one function that you would fulfill, there will be nothing else
the Holy Spirit will not arrange for you without your effort. He
will go before you making straight your path, and leaving in your
way no stones to trip on, and no obstacles to bar your way. Not
one seeming difficulty but will melt away before you reach it. You
need take thought for nothing, careless of everything except the
only purpose that you would fulfill.*

-A Course in Miracles

We know where you are. We know how to find you. We know what
you are like and how you can best be used. We know how to bring
happiness into your life and how to use you as a catalyst to bring
greater joy to others. We were sent to you specifically and We are totally
prepared for the assignment.

But you have got to relax and get out of the way while still
continuing to show up for your life. We know this is difficult for you
because you tend to think that if you show up, you need to take control
and have a plan and get busy making things work.

Slow down miracle worker. Let Us do our job. Tune into the energy more frequently rather than trying to CREATE the energy that you think would be best. Stop micro-managing a meaningless life. The meaning in life does not come from your ideas about what should be happening. The meaningful moments in life cannot be manipulated or controlled. You simply show up for them, prepared to follow the inner-directions given; prepared to give and receive without closing off your valve.

Let go of promoting and begin to experience the effortless attracting power of JOY.

160

Enter the Field of Grace

o o o o o o o o o o o o o o o o o o o o o o o o o o o o o o o o o

What could you not accept, if you but knew that everything that happens, all events, past, present and to come, are gently planned by One Whose only purpose is your good?

-A Course in Miracles

You are forever in a state of grace. It is only your awareness of it that shifts and changes. Most often you experience that grace when your defenses are finally down - in moments of tremendous grief and sorrow or in moments of transcendence. But the grace is there all the time.

You may have heard one of Our teachers tell you to *"let law of attraction sort out all the details"* but we are telling that that is still a somewhat stressful place of mental efforting. You would do much better to allow grace to sort out all the details for you. There is much less thinking involved, less mental effort, less working through contrast. It is a place where you are no longer working to get the situations and people to be pleasing to you - instead, in the state of grace you've become a much more pleasable being. You will find yourself less rigid and controlling. You will find that you are expanding and enjoying things that you never thought you would, or that you didn't in the past.

The Universe Itself will be bringing to you wonderful people, places and experiences that you would never even known to ask for or to consider. Grace gently changes you in surprising and delightful ways. Let grace work out all the details for you and see how much more peaceful and gentle you become as you release the need to control that which can never really be controlled anyhow. And it is in those moments that you allow yourself to experience grace that you are most likely to actually see and hear Us. We have appeared to many many people in the moments in which they consciously or unconsciously gave up control somewhere along the path.

161

International "Give Everyone a Fucking Break" Day!

o o o o o o o o o o o o o o o o o o o o o o o o o o o o o o o o o o o

Give them a place of refuge, prepared for them where once a desert was. And everyone you welcome will bring love with him from Heaven for you.

-A Course in Miracles

You have no idea what anyone is going through. The woman who is driving so unsatisfactorily in front of you may have just been given the news that the cancer has spread. The very slow-moving bank teller may have just found out that the woman he is engaged to is having second thoughts about the marriage. Even the person closest to you who tells you everything may not be telling you everything about the terror that is gripping him right now.

You may be feeling very oceanic today and be ready to practice loving-kindness to all creatures great and small out of the abundance of your own heart. We would love that and you will feel wonderful because of it. But, you may have your own issues going on today and not feel quite so full of that cosmic love, in which case We recommend that you simply remember to give everyone a fucking break today. Just back off on evaluating and judging how they are doing. You don't need to know why they are acting as they are or why they so desperately need a break. It doesn't matter that they don't "deserve" it. Do it for your own sake. Do it in honor of this special holiday.

Please, please, please include yourself in this practice. Look in the mirror and say, *"Guess what friend? I'm giving you a fucking break all day long today - just because! No judging, no criticizing, no trying to manipulate and control you or telling you how you should be! I'm letting you off the hook today and treating you with patience, kindness and generosity. Just because!"*

162

No One is Stopping You

o o o o o o o o o o o o o o o o o o o o o o o o o o o o o o o o

There is no order of difficulty in miracles. One is not "bigger" or "harder" than another. They are all the same. All expressions of love are maximal.

-A Course in Miracles

No one stops you but yourself. No one is holding you back except you by believing the thoughts that testify to limitation and finite resources.

You have an opportunity every moment to hold yourself back or to take a step forward in faith and optimism that within you is all that you will need to handle whatever comes up.

Don't rush yourself, but don't let it all pass you by either simply because you are telling yourself a story of what you think is possible.

Miracle workers are not interested in past precedent. Records are shattered first in the mind and **then** in the world.

163

You Are Not Broken

○ ○

What you do comes from what you think.

-A Course in Miracles

You are not broken. You are not damaged, nor are you damaged goods. You simply have some habit patterns which are consistent with the story you tell yourself about "you."

Nothing is stopping you except some old habits which no longer serve you. You may have created them in the past in order to survive something fearful, but it's now time to let them go. By this time, you are probably well aware of what they are. Don't let it upset you or defeat you or get you down. It's simply information about the ways in which you tell yourself a story that creates a habit which sabotages certain of your efforts. The REAL habit is not behavioral anyhow - it is a thought habit and the thought creates the behavior. Once you are aware of the habits which are sabotaging you, take your attention entirely AWAY from them because We are about focusing on solutions, not problems.

For instance, if you hold yourself back from participating in some area of life somehow, that is simply an old behavioral habit that is based on a deep habit of thought. Only YOU are holding you back from walking right up to that person, group or situation and taking part in it.

You tell yourself a story of limitation, you believe it, and then it creates certain behaviors. Most often, it is a story of how you are broken, damaged, inadequate or that you will somehow be overwhelmed and swallowed up by something beyond your control or that you are too overwhelming and intense for the world to handle. But that is just an old story which is not being questioned in the present moment. It is not being challenged or changed.

All that is really needed is to begin very slowly, very patiently, to develop some new habits. The best way to dissolve an old habit is by replacing it with a new one. A NEW thought neutralizes an old opposing thought. It is a bio-chemical process.

You can begin with the simple thought of *"Nothing is stopping me from taking the next indicated step forward. I can do this one little thing right now and it doesn't mean anything one way or the other. No praise and no blame. It's just a choice and I am choosing to think a new thought and to tell a new better story. Whatever happens, I can handle it."*

164

Practice Good Listening

o o o o o o o o o o o o o o o o o o o o o o o o o o o o o o o o

Whenever you meet anyone, it is a holy encounter.

-A Course in Miracles

Slow down miracle worker. Learn to listen gently and carefully to your sisters and brothers.

Be patient. Listen rather than interpret. Be present. Really listen to exactly what is being said without imposing your story onto it. Too often you project your own biography onto others in order to "cut to the chase" because it eases your own discomfort.

Someone asks for prayer and you give them advice instead. Someone asks for a little help and instead you do it for them. This dishonors the other person and shows that you are not really present, not listening to them but are imposing your own story onto them.

You are always free to say yes or no to anyone once you really HEAR what it is that THEY are saying but if you do not take the time to really listen, you miss the true intimacy of life which is the Holy Instant.

Acknowledgements

o o o o o o o o o o o o o o o o o o o o o o o o o o o o o o o o

Can love be far behind a grateful heart and a thankful mind?

-A Course in Miracles

I want to thank everybody in my life – in particular the students who show up every Sunday in San Diego and once a month in Santa Barbara with a HUGE thank you to the donors and those who listen to the CD's every week. Special thanks to Park Manor Suites and staff as well as Unity of Santa Barbara.

I won't mention all the names because certainly I would leave someone very important out inadvertently. I appreciate you all very very much and you are on my daily prayer and gratitude lists forever.

Suggested Reading List:

A Course in Miracles – published by the Foundation for Inner-Peace
www.acim.org

Loving What Is – Byron Katie

Love and the Law – Ernest Holmes

Living by Grace – Joel Goldsmith

Steering by Starlight – Martha Beck

The Four Spiritual Laws of Prosperity – Edwene Gaines

The Dark Side of the Light Chasers – Debbie Ford

Ask And It Is Given – Esther and Jerry Hicks

About the Author

Jacob Glass is a spiritual author, teacher and international super-model. He lives and teaches in Southern California and if you happen to see him out at coffee some morning before 10 a.m. you should avoid him at all costs.

www.jacobglass.com